Miracle of Marriage

Douglas Weiss, Ph.D.

MIRACLE OF MARRIAGE
Copyright © 2011 by Douglas Weiss
Published by Discovery Press
P.O. Box 51055
Colorado Springs, CO 80949

Unless otherwise noted, all Scripture quotations are from the Holy Bible, New International Version. Copyright 1973, 1978, 1984, International Bible Society. Used by permission.

All Rights reserved
Printed in the United States of America
ISBN # 978-1-881292-33-3
No portion of this material may be reproduced in any form or by any means without written permission of the author.

Edited by Anita K.
Cover Design by Janelle Evangelides
Interior Design by Jamie Dodd

Chapters

Introduction	5
1. A Different View	9
2. The Miracle Process	25
3. Work	49
4. Miracle is Progressive	69
5. Maintaining the Miracle	95
6. Protecting the Miracle	113
7. Principles	141
8. Purpose of Marriage	155
9. Their Maker	183
10. How to Change your Spouse	201
11. Three Roles of Marriage	229
12. Pitch of Praise	251
13. 10 Commandments for Marriage	273
Appendix	305

Introduction

I was sitting in an airport, on my way to speak at a marriage conference in Canada. I had already spoken to couples at this church last year so they wanted something a little different this time for those that were attending again. That was no problem. I offer three different marriage conferences based upon the three marriage books I have written. I was confident we would be able to do something different.

Sitting in the airport I asked God for something different. He told me to go read a very familiar passage in the Bible. I was tempted not to read it, but I decided to obey as I had nothing better to do at the time anyway.

I opened my Bible to this familiar passage. It was a passage I have written about and preached on hundreds of times. When I read it something happened... revelation. I was wowed like I have only been wowed a few times in my life. I discovered revelation that I have never seen before nor have I ever heard it preached before and it was jumping off the page at me.

I could not even stay seated I was so excited. I went to the conference and those that heard this very fresh revelation on marriage were wowed as well. The pages ahead of you are revolutionary. I have run these thoughts by well known Christian television artists, as well as seasoned ministers that have been in ministry for more than 40 years, and they told me that they had never heard this insight before.

I hope that what has happened to me after this insight soaked in happens to every man and woman who reads this book. I was able to see the true miracle of marriage. I was able to more appreciate God and my wife Lisa, my wife of over 25 years. I have been touched and changed and I hope you are as well.

Douglas Weiss, Ph.D.

"In the beginning God created"

A Different View 1

"In the beginning God created"...I always thought that was a great opening statement to the best book ever written. In Genesis we are introduced to God's massive creation.

Most of us have read the story and some of us older people (before computers) may have even seen this great story on the high tech presentation called the felt board. However you were introduced to the creation story, I believe you are going to learn something so incredibly new that it can literally change the way you read this account the rest of your life.

I know that may sound impossible. What could you possibly learn from that scripture that you don't already know about creation? However, being a Christian now for more than thirty years and having two degrees in Bible I continue to learn and I see this story differently ever since I've listened to what God was trying to reveal to me in the creation story.

Hold on, we are going to travel through some familiar ground that is foundational to your final destination. Let's begin with, "In the beginning God created..."

"And God said, "Let there be light," and there was light."

Genesis 1:3

God starts his creation by making heaven and earth. I'm really glad he did that. On a mountain top in Colorado, I love how I can see so much of His creation and I enjoy it. I have been blessed to be able to travel around the country and see many of His other amazing creations as well.

In Genesis 1:3, God decides to create light. He called the light day and it's wonderful to be able to see all He creates because of this light he has made for us. He continues to recreate the sky in new ways every day. I'm sitting on a plane this very moment as I write this and flying through his sky is an awesome experience. Seeing the oceans of clouds or the sun rise while traveling in a plane is a delight and we see this all because he created light.

In Genesis 1:9, He creates the dry ground. For all my hiker, biker and trail blazer friends the dry ground is heavenly for them. It gets more exciting because He starts to make food from this creation. Interestingly, God created vegetation first including the trees, many types of grass and the many tasty things we randomly throw on a salad plate. I guess it took forethought to create food before He creates the one who eats the food. As a guy I think about those important things.

Then God backs out of the earth for a moment to create the sun, moon, stars. Just think about the amazing power of our God! When I step outside on a clear night, His star creation is amazing and inspiring. A God that big is truly awesome.

God then goes back to creating on the earth: fish and birds and then all of the other creatures. So now the earth is getting more active with the animals walking around and eating some of those great vegetables.

> *"Then God said, "Let us make man in our image, in our likeness, and let them rule over the fish of the sea and the birds of the air, over the livestock, over all the earth, and over all the creatures that move along the ground."*
>
> *Genesis 1:26*

Soon we are introduced for the first time to a heaven in the trinity in Genesis 1. God interprets those creation events by talking to His son and the Holy Spirit in verse 26, "Then God said, 'Let us make mankind in our image, in our likeness, so that they may rule over the fish in the sea and the birds in the sky, over the livestock and all the wild animals, and over all the creatures that move along the ground.'"

This is truly curious because at this time God pauses and talks before He gets started with the creation of man and woman. At the end of chapter one it says, "So God created man in His own image."

Honestly when we read this passage, there are several points I would like us to highlight before going to God's main event in the garden. First and foremost, God did the creating. No man was involved. He receives the glory for all He creates on earth. Each step in creation becomes more complex. First light, vegetation, fish, birds, creatures and then man and woman. I don't think it's any stretch at all to say creation became more intricate and more like the one who made them as God moved through this creation process.

Moving on through the foundations of creation I want to take you to an amazing view of His final creation. As you read through chapter one it is interesting to me that each of these wonderful creations were only given a line or two. God created the heavens, and then God created the earth. Even man and woman are only given one sentence for their complex creation.

It's at this time that something happens. It's kind of like watching a movie that you have seen several times. Our brains turn off after reading that God created man and woman. Nothing could be further from the truth. All of Genesis chapter one was a warm up for what he was about to create. His masterpiece was still not created.

For this event, God dedicates several scriptures to magnify His final creation. In this creation process He starts with two beings, but let's slow down and read the rest of the story. It's one of the best in the history of the world.

> "The Lord God said, "It is not good for the man to be alone. I will make a helper suitable for him."
> Genesis 2:18

In Genesis chapter two we see Adam alone working in the garden and naming the animals. He has been working on this for a while. Nobody knows how long but it was long enough for God to feel sorry for him that he didn't have a mate. In verse 18 God says, "It is not good for the man to be alone. I will make him a helper suitable for him."

Just a quick side note, there is not a man reading this that doesn't know it is not good for man to be alone. All men remember this ache of singleness because we needed a connection with a permanent mate. Some of our decisions definitely need refining. Lastly, I don't know if you have ever been in a guy's dorm, but there are smells and things there that you will never experience anywhere else. So I think we could all agree with God that it is not good for man to be alone.

Now here we'll go into the expanded version of a creation. Remember in Genesis chapter one it was just that God created man and woman. Now God goes into detail.

You know the story of how He puts man to sleep (that way he couldn't have an opinion). He took a rib to create Eve. Now hit the pause button for a moment. Adam was created, but by himself he could not procreate. Eve was created and she could not procreate. You see, God was going to take these two parts, these two separate beings and He was going to create his final masterpiece, marriage!

> *"That is why a man leaves his father and mother and is united to his wife, and they become one flesh."*
> *Genesis 2:24*

In Genesis 2:24 it says that God brought her to the man. God made marriage not Adam; God brought her to the man. Then to continue that this marriage was by itself a final creation He says, "and they will be become one flesh."

Marriage, not Eve was God's final creation in the garden! Not that woman isn't amazing and truly more complex and beautiful enough, but marriage is even more complex and looks more like the Godhead than any other creation on planet earth or in the known galaxy.

God's ultimate creation is truly in His image. The Trinity is three beings living in an awesome amount of love and unity. They were creating a complex relationship of three on earth as it is in Heaven. In Heaven you have God the Father, God the Son, and God the Holy Spirit. In marriage you have God, man and woman. On earth the final creation of God is a trinity.

He is smack in the middle of this family photograph. His final creation in the sinless garden was this triune relationship between God, Adam, and Eve. Wow! I don't know about you, but that changes the whole creation story. Creation didn't end with man and woman. Although we were created in His image we're not the final act of creation, marriage was.

I think this is why the enemy of our soul hates Christian marriages so much. He lived with the trinity. He knew God the Father, the Son, and the Holy Spirit. He worshiped them with all his might before being rejected and sent to earth. A Christian marriage that truly has God as a real person in it, is just like looking at the Trinity.

Take a moment and think deeply about your marriage as a trinity, a triunion on earth as it is in Heaven. Your marriage is the very symbol of God on earth. Your marriage is what has the most potential to reflect our God to those around us. Your marriage is a whole and unique creation of the Almighty God. Your marriage is His masterpiece.

I hope you enjoyed the re-landscaping of the creation story. It has changed my life to know that marriage is God's final creation. When this is understood, no man gets credit for marriage. Marriage is something God does. Marriage is something that clearly has three people in it. Marriage as the final creation can now reproduce.

Adam by himself could not reproduce; Eve by herself could not reproduce. Now as a triune marriage they can reproduce, not only children, but these seeds can grow up, and with God create a new trinity. Your triune marriage is a life-giving trinity that can go on until the end of time. One trinity (Adam, Eve and God) has spawned an entire human race. Your trinity can be a tree of life for so many as time goes on. That's why your trinity is so important. There are ingredients in your trinity that can go down for a thousand years or more for better or worse.

I love that I get no credit for my marriage. That it was truly God who created Lisa, and if I might add, He did a marvelous job. God then brought her to me and over time He created this marriage. He sustains this marriage because it truly is His creation, not mine. God, Lisa and I are a unique creation.

You, your spouse and God are a unique creation of God. The three of you have a unique story of how God created your Adam with all his strengths, foibles, weaknesses and adorable features. Likewise your Eve has an amazing story of how God has created her: her beauty, wisdom, idiosyncrasies and weaknesses. Then there is also the story of God in your marriage. Through this lens, you can see it is a miracle. When I see my marriage as a unique miracle, I realize, I didn't do it. Lisa didn't do it, God did it.

So as you go through these pages on the Miracle of Marriage my prayer is that you start where God started. Your marriage is His miracle. In the continuing pages we will expand on this miracle but for now take a moment and really let it soak in your heart that your marriage is a creation of God Almighty, the same God who created galaxies and creatures, also created your marriage. Your marriage is truly a miracle.

Your marriage was a miracle in progress before you ever met

The Miracle Process 2

Many reading this book have had one of the most amazing experiences of a lifetime. No, I am not talking about walking down the aisle; I am talking about something that is really beyond words. It's a supernatural experience. I am talking about the day you hold your first child.

This baby, being so small, so fragile, creates some of the most powerful feelings inside of you that you will ever experience. I think that's how God feels when you walk down the aisle before friends and family and say those life changing words, "I do."

I can imagine why. He feels so proud, amazed and happy as He builds His final creation, your marriage. This creation is still young and doesn't know much, but has amazing potential and brings amazing joy to His heart.

Similar to the moment of holding a newborn which is amazing alone, marriage also has many moments that lead up to and allow you to finally experience the miracle moment. There is the inception moment of the child, then the moments wondering if you are pregnant before you even decide to tell your husband. Then the moment comes to share the exciting news. Medical tests follow to verify this information along with vitamins and doctor's visits.

Remember conversations about what color the baby's room was going to be and what equipment you were going to get your future child? How many hours went into picking a name? Sonograms, cravings, mood swings, thoughts about the ever expanding body, the baby's health, and bed rest followed.

Getting closer to the due date came with Lamaze classes, planning for the hospital visit, bags packed and the moment the wife says, "It's time." The baby arrives and this new little face gets to see you and the world around it, what a glorious moment.

In the same way that there were so many moments that leads up to the birth of your child, there were also many moments that lead you up to the miracle of your marriage.

Your marriage was a miracle in progress before you ever met. Before Adam ever could conceive of an idea called Eve, God was behind the scenes planning. He was training Adam to have a relationship with God. This was a relationship Adam would deeply need before he ever met a woman.

Adam would need his relationship with God through every stage of his marriage. God was building a foundation of intimacy with Him so Adam could use these skills in his marriage with Eve. God also was giving Adam work to do. Adam had the task of maintaining the Garden and naming the animals.

God was making sure Adam had the work ethic needed in his marriage. Marriage is work and it is needed by both the man and the woman. Man must be able to get through difficult days, solve frustrating problems and have the ability to persist to be the best fit for marriage. God knew what He was doing when He gave men challenges.

God gave Adam another skill prior to giving him the gift of a woman. Another skill that Adam received prior to Eve was creativity. Adam had to name everything from the aardvark to the zebra. That is a huge task requiring an amazing amount of creativity, intellect and memory so as not to repeat any. Most of us today couldn't even list a few hundred creatures that have already been named.

God was starting his miracle of marriage by placing skills in Adam for the preparation of the final creation. God also spent time with Eve creating an intimate relationship with her before giving Adam to her. She definitely would also need this primary, intimate relationship with God as an ingredient for an intimate triune marriage.

Let's go back in time so you can chronicle your own unique miracle of marriage. On this journey you will both need a pen so you can fill in the many blanks that only you can answer about your miracle process. Let's start with Adam's journey toward his miracle of marriage.

Adam (the husband)

What were some of the strengths and weaknesses of your dad?

Strengths _____

_____

Weaknesses _____

_____

What were some of the strengths and weaknesses of your mom?

Strengths _____

_____

Weaknesses _____

_____

What did you learn from your birth order? _____

_____

_____

_____

What did you learn from you family of origin about:

Solving problems? _____

_____

Taking responsibility? _____

_____

Fear? _____

_____

Anger? _____

_____

Accepting or judging others? _____

_____

Sex? _____

_____

Money? _____

_____

How to treat a woman? _____

_____

Who's the boss and why? _____

_____

God? _____
_____

Pets? _____
_____

Parenting roles? _____
_____

Education? _____
_____

What are the top three accomplishments you have had prior to graduation?

1. _____
_____

2. _____
_____

3. _____
_____

What are three of your worst moments prior to graduating high school?

1. _____

2. _____

3. _____

List 3 life changing experiences you had prior to age 18?

1. _____

2. _____

3. _____

Adam (the husband) when you were a young adult (after high school until married or 30 years old). What did you learn about:

Money? _____

Responsibility? _____

_____

Sex? _____

_____

Your fears? _____

_____

Anger? _____

_____

Humility? _____

_____

Submission? _____

_____

Solving problems? _____

_____

Accepting/judging others? _____

_____

How to treat a woman? _____

_____

Who's the boss and why? _____

_____

What were your top 3 accomplishments as a young adult (exclude meeting your wife-God did that)?

1. _____

_____

2. _____

_____

3. _____

_____

What were three of your worst experiences as a young adult?

1. _____

_____

2. _____

_____

3. _____

_____

What were three life changing experiences as a young adult?

1. _____

2. _____
_____

3. _____
_____

Adam (the husband), I want you to take what you wrote down and share these with your wife. You see you had many experiences prior to your miracle of marriage. Sharing these can be helpful and even bond you together, even a little more than before.

Eve (the wife)

1. What were some of the strengths and weaknesses of your dad?

Strengths _____

_____

Weaknesses _____

_____

What were some of the strengths and weaknesses of your mom?

Strengths _____

_____

Weaknesses _____

_____

What did you learn from your birth order? _____

_____

_____

_____

What did you learn from you family of origin about:

Solving problems? _____

_____

Taking responsibility? _____

_____

Fear? _____

_____

Anger? _____
_____

Accepting or judging others? _____
_____

Sex? _____
_____

Money? _____
_____

How to treat a man? _____
_____

Who's the boss and why? _____
_____

God? _____
_____

Pets? _____
_____

Parenting roles? _____
_____

Education? _____
_____

What are the top three accomplishments you have had prior to graduation?

1. _____

_____

2. _____

_____

3. _____

_____

What are three of your worst moments prior to graduating high school?

1. _____

_____

2. _____

_____

3. _____

_____

List 3 life changing experiences you had prior to age 18?

1. _____

_____

2. _____

3. _____

Eve (the wife) when you were a young adult (after high school until married or 30).
What did you learn about:

Money? _____

Responsibility? _____

Sex? _____

Your fears? _____

Anger? _____

Humility? _____

Submission? _____

_____

Solving problems? _____

_____

Accepting/judging others? _____

_____

How to treat a man? _____

_____

Who's the boss and why? _____

_____

What were your top 3 accomplishments as a young adult (exclude meeting your wife-God did that)?

1. _____

_____

2. _____

_____

3. _____

_____

What were three of your worst experiences as a young adult?

1. _____

_____

2. _____

_____

3. _____

_____

What were three life changing experiences as a young adult?

1. _____

_____

2. _____

_____

3. _____

_____

Eve (the wife), I want you to take what you wrote down and share these with your husband. You see you had many experiences prior to your miracle of marriage. Sharing these can be helpful and even bond you both together even a little more than before.

In the rest of the chapter, I want you both to work together and fill in the blanks. This part of the journey has to do with God bringing you together.
How far away from each other were you growing up?

A block, a city, a state, a country?

_____

_____

What was your first initial impression of him?

_____

_____

What was your first initial impression of her?

_____

_____

How long during the dating process did you know that they were the one for you and explain:

Adam: _____

_____

Eve: _____

_____

List 5 things that really attracted you to the other person.

Adam
1. _____
2. _____
3. _____
4. _____
5. _____

Eve
1. _____
2. _____
3. _____
4. _____
5. _____

What were some of the challenges you personally had to work through to consider marrying them?

Adam: _____

_____

Eve: _____
_____

How did you overcome these challenges?
Adam: _____
_____
Eve: _____
_____

How and where did the proposal occur? _____
_____
_____
_____

How did you figure out:
Where to get married? _____
_____
Who would be the best people in the wedding party?
_____

The Miracle Process 45

The honeymoon? _____
_____

What were some of the feelings you had on the wedding day?

Adam: _____
_____

Eve: _____
_____

After the vows and the kiss, how did you feel?

Adam: _____
_____

Eve: _____
_____

What did you learn about God creating your miracle of marriage in this process? Take a moment to talk about it. I find couples that can remember their story as a miracle, can also recognize that God can continue to write their story throughout their marriage during challenging circumstances of marriage.

When we receive a miracle, we are humbled at the awareness that we are not innately worthy of the miracle God just graced us with, and it is apparent.

Work 3

Let's go back to our conversation about expecting a baby and the moments during and after this life giving experience. The wife is sweating, crying, and pushing when the little amazing child of God is delivered. After the doctor or nurse cleans up this miracle of God, the parents are handed the newborn child.

I don't know about you but when I held both of my children at birth I had several really strong feelings invade my masculine soul. First, I was very sure there was a very big, amazing, creative, all powerful God who gives the gift of life. It took every ounce of self restraint not to break out into full worship of the Most High God right there in the delivery room.

Secondly, I was largely aware that He alone was God, and I was not. I knew other than an infinitely small contribution I had nothing to do with this amazing child I was holding. I didn't make this child grow, give substance, choose their eye or hair color, or their personality. In other words, I was convinced there was a God, and I was not Him.

Thirdly, I felt humbled, even unworthy of this miracle I was holding. I don't know about you, but throughout my Christian walk I have received many miracles. I have been healed and delivered many times from circumstances. I have been supernaturally provided for numerous times as I have been matured by God. Like you, I have been in need of a miracle many times. Sometimes I would fast, pray, cry out to God, get broken, worship, read the Word, share with others until the miracle would finally happen. When we receive a miracle, we are humbled at the awareness that we are not innately worthy of the miracle God just graced us with, and it is apparent.

When you hold a child, you know you hold a miracle. When you hold a marriage you also hold in your hand and heart a bonafide, one of a kind, special delivery miracle from God to you. That's not only a feeling that your marriage is a bonafide miracle of God, it's the truth. God created marriage; God created your marriage and your marriage is a miracle.

I find couples who see their marriage as a miracle have totally different core beliefs about marriage than those that are not aware that their marriage is a miracle. Those that are not consistently cognizant that their marriage is a real miracle and a gift to them have totally different ideas or beliefs about their marriage. Just like those of us who do not believe our life is a God created miracle believe and behave totally in contradiction to the fact that God created us for His purpose and pleasure.

Let's put this in perspective for a moment. Each child of God that is born is amazing. As long as you can still see the amazing in your child you will treat them as the miracle they really are even on the challenging days.

In the below space, write out, without asking for help, ten amazing qualities about your spouse:

Adam's Amazing Qualities
1._____
2._____
3._____
4._____
5._____

Eve's Amazing Qualities
1._____
2._____
3._____
4._____
5._____

6. _____   6. _____
7. _____   7. _____
8. _____   8. _____
9. _____   9. _____
10. _____   10. _____

Now I want you to do something that you may not have done in a while. Write down qualities about yourself that are not so wonderful, actually some things may not be that nice at all (also, don't ask for help).

Adam (for himself)   *Eve (for herself)*

1. _____   1. _____
2. _____   2. _____
3. _____   3. _____
4. _____   4. _____
5. _____   5. _____
6. _____   6. _____
7. _____   7. _____
8. _____   8. _____

Work 53

9._____ 9._____
10._____ 10._____

Now let me ask you a serious question. It's a question I ask regularly when doing one of my marriage conferences. What is it about you that makes you innately worthy to be loved, served and celebrated for fifty to seventy-five years? My answer is nothing. There is nothing that makes me worthy of Lisa's love, devotion, acts of service and just the joy of her presence. I am in the miracle of marriage, like all the other miracles God had chosen to grace me with, I am not worthy of the miracle.

When you see this final creation of God that you get to participate in, it affects your attitude within your marriage. When you see this miracle of marriage as a gift to you from God, your marriage becomes holy. That's why I think it's proper to call it holy matrimony because your marriage and mine are evidence of a divine presence and manifestation of His miraculous hand on earth. This view of marriage is a core belief.

The last characteristic of someone who understands that their marriage is a miracle will have to be explained in context. Let's go back again to holding your miracle child in your arms for the first time. There is something that happened in my heart when holding my children, Hadassah and Jubal, that I believe happens to almost everyone who holds their newborn child. There was an overwhelming feeling that my life now is about them, serving them and making sure their needs are met. They now have a really high value and my needs really will have to be reevaluated in the context of this new miracle that just arrived.

When you truly understand that you are participating

in a miracle called marriage, your heart goes out to meet your spouse's needs. They become a very high priority and your needs are to be considered in the bigger picture. Your life to a large degree becomes about them.

> *I have observed the following characteristics consistently in those who value their marriage as a miracle:*
> 1) *a sense of awe,*
> 2) *a sense of unworthiness of the miracle,*
> 3) *a sense of holiness, and*
> 4) *knowing it's about the other person*

I have observed the following characteristics consistently in those who value their marriage as a miracle: 1) a sense of awe, 2) a sense of unworthiness of the miracle, 3) a sense of holiness, and 4) knowing it's about the other person. I wish every Christian marriage had these core beliefs, however that is not the case.

Let's walk through some characteristics of couples who do not fully believe their marriage is a miracle. If these characteristics seem familiar, don't worry, we are all a work in progress, but for everybody's sake, I would encourage you to progress.

When someone does not believe their marriage is a miracle, a separate creation of God, they walk in various degrees of being deceived. What I mean by deceived is we believe something God doesn't. A deceived person could look at a child and see him or her as a number, instead of a miracle made in the image of God. In the same way, a married person can be deceived by sensing their marriage as less than this amazing miracle. The four characteristics of a married person who has a degree of deception are as follows; firstly, a married person with deception has no awe of the marriage itself. To them, it's just a marriage. This person is rarely aware of all the miracles it took for them to get married or to stay married. A deceived person might live their life as if their marriage is a legal arrangement, a mutual living situation or even worse, something to be distained.

Secondly, a deceived person in marriage actually believes and behaves as if they are innately worthy of someone dedicating their life to them. They have attitudes that others are there to serve them and make them happy. Now I know that sounds ridiculous, but I have seen Christians who actually believe this. It's like believing somehow you earned marriage instead of receiving it as a miracle. Entitlement is common when this deception is present.

Thirdly, a deceived person in a marriage will not be able to see anything holy in a marriage. Their understanding is that God is a real person but He has nothing to do with marriage. They believe there is no accountability for their actions toward their spouse. Yes, I'm talking about Christian men and women. They go to church, quote scripture, but remain cruel to their spouse. Their deception disconnects the value of their spouse as a child of God. Deception also keeps them disconnected between their cruelty and their Christianity. I often tell those with this level of self deception that they are as close to God as their behavior toward your spouse. If their behavior is godly toward their spouse then they are most likely close to God and vice-versa. When they want to blame their spouse, I quickly say, "Jesus didn't blame the centurions who crucified Him but instead chose to love them." He was congruent on the cross as we hope to be when we are dying to ourselves in marriage. It breaks my heart when I see a religious man or woman who is so deceived about themselves and their behavior toward a child of God, their spouse. The person who thinks that their marriage is not holy doesn't have to value their vows of love, honor, and cherish nor take the vows of fidelity very seriously. Since they don't acknowledge their marriage as a gift from God it can easily be disregarded. Also, their belief that God is not intricately involved in their marriage, encourages their ugly attitudes of rudeness, unkindness, neglect and abuse to not get addressed since there is no accountability for their behaviors.

The deceived person in a marriage does not contemplate that they will stand before an awesome God and answer for their behavior toward their spouse. They don't fear God in their relationship to their spouse. This disconnect allows bad things to keep growing and instead of dying to themselves their flesh continues to grow. I know many times God had to remind me of who and who's Lisa is. She is His favored daughter, even before she was my wife.

Fourthly, the deceived married person has never really felt the call to serve in their marriage. They are selfish and often neglectful of their spouse's needs, desires, or dreams. This deceived person goes days, weeks, years, or even decades without really considering how to love and serve their spouse. This person's self absorption keeps them oblivious to the gift and miracle they are married to. This unawareness allows them to be irresponsible to see or serve their spouse.

Often the person who is deceived in this manner has reported feeling resentful that their spouse has a need. Their spouse's need itself frustrates them. Why? Because a spouse's legitimate need is a holy call to service. This service kills our flesh and makes us like Christ. So the deceived person makes their spouse's needs illegitimate or weak so they don't have to respond to a call to serve.

My experience is that God places needs in your spouse that are parallel to your greatest weakness. This demands you to really grow to be able to optimize your miracle of marriage.

Suppose you have a husband who knows his wife likes to be physically touched. This need is just the way God made her and when she is touched, given a back rub or a foot rub a few times a week she is happy and able to do amazing things. When she is untouched she has various known predicable symptoms that He is well aware.

A deceived man blames, ignores, minimizes or shames his wife for this need. God is calling him to die to himself and give touch freely and regularly so he can be more free and Christ like and his wife can flourish in His design.

I've known deceived Christian women who deny sex

to their husbands and blame them for being cranky. I know deceived men who deny emotional and spiritual intimacy to their wife and wonder why they don't want sex. In both cases the spouse is not responding to the call of their spouse's needs and to serve them to see how powerful this miracle of marriage could truly be if both died to themselves.

You don't have to be a Christian very long to know you can be saved and yet in some areas of your life be fully or partially deceived, whether it be financially, sexually, in parenting, or your work ethics. So let's place these four ideas next to each other to see where you might currently be. Viewing this side by side can help assess where you are, but regardless you can totally walk in the revelation that your marriage is a complete miracle of God.

You may want to take a few moments and evaluate what you really believe about marriage. To do this

Miracle	Deceived
1. In awe of marriage	1. No awe of Marriage
2. Unworthy to be married	2. Thinks they are innately worthy of marriage
3. Marriage is holy	3. Marriage is not holy
4. About serving a spouse	4. About serving me

I want to give you a solid principle you can use to assess yourself as to what you truly believe about marriage. This principle is what I call believing behavior.

Don't believe about your marriage just what you philosophically or theologically believe, rather look at your attitudes and behaviors in your marriage. Here are some ideas of what I mean about believing behaviors.

For example if you are in awe of your marriage, you will have a general attitude of thankfulness to God for your spouse. You will also be inclined to be more patient because you're in a God deal. However if you are not in awe of your marriage, you will tend to be more critical of your spouse and generally be ungrateful.

If you really believe you are unworthy of your miracle, you will pitch in. You're part of the team. The dishes and laundry are yours whether you're a man or a woman. When you feel that you are worthy of your spouse, you have entitlement and you have the behavior of focusing on what your spouse doesn't do right. Actually most people I meet who feel worthy are not only critical, they are usually less happy than the person who really believes they are unworthy of the miracle they are married to.

The behavior of a person who believes their marriage

is holy would be praying together. The person who believes their marriage is holy, also feels convicted when they sin toward their spouse and will tend to be confessing their sin to their spouse fairly consistently. A person's behavior if they think their marriage is not holy is disrespectful and often demeaning toward their spouse. They also tend to blame their spouse for their own behavior and minimize it even when they are clearly wrong.

The behavior of a person who has really felt the call to serve their spouse is consistent. They know what needs to be done, not just around the house, but what needs to be done for their spouse to feel loved or special. They serve, not to be served, but rather because it's what's right in view of this amazing miracle they have received from God.

A person who really believes the marriage is about them is inconsistent. They often complain about even doing small things around the house for their spouse. They have an attitude of being inconvenienced when their spouse or family member has need of them. I think you get the idea of believing your behavior.

Behaviors always tell you the truth. So think through this so you can have a healthy evaluation of what you really believe about whether your marriage is a bonifide miracle of God.

The very first idea that comes to my mind when I heard the words "and they will become one flesh" is that whatever this process is, the one thing it is not is instant.

Miracle is Progressive 4

Let's travel back in time to the Garden of Eden for a moment. The place in this story I want to visit is after God brings the woman to the man. In Genesis 2:24 God says, "And they will become one flesh." This statement clearly alludes to God creating something entirely new, the creation of a new flesh from two individuals so they can become this new creation called marriage. He also alludes to the fact that this creation, this masterpiece is not at all instantaneous.

Let's look back to the miracle of a child. When this child is conceived and God breathes his spark of life into this child, it is a miracle. If you have ever had the experience of seeing a sonogram of a child in the womb you definitely see the miracle as it moves with its little hands and feet, eyes and beating heart. When the child is born, and as miraculous as that is, it's just another stage of this amazing progressive miracle called a child. The baby coo's and cries and eventually becomes a toddler. Then the miracle continues to grow into a preschooler, a student all the way through high school. Each of these stages is full of developmental tasks, challenges, peers, successes and teachable moments.

This miracle goes on to college or work. They begin to find their way in life. They get married, have a family. You see, the whole lifespan is a miracle form conception until death. A life is a miracle gift from God. This miracle called life is definitely progressive and continues to develop over decades.

Now let's see if becoming one flesh in light of this miracle of marriage is also progressive. The very first idea that comes to my mind when I heard the words "and they will become one flesh" is that whatever this process is, the one thing it is not is instant. Wouldn't it be amazing if the moment the groom kissed the bride they would instantly become one. I'm not sure what that would look like, but wow, wouldn't that be amazing. Obviously no one could take that level of transformation instantly.

Imagine a bizarre scene in a movie where two characters merge their heads, bodies and limbs and become some sort of creature. This would make weddings a whole lot more interesting. "I wonder what they will look like as they merge, will they look more like him, her or Uncle Bob?" Thank God His idea is Kingdom and over time. However, if you do get to observe a marriage of fifty or sixty years in length of time, you can see a oneness in which they are both more Christ like.

Actually as far as a lifetime goes, I think it's easily fifty to seventy-five years until you become fully one flesh. Along the way there are signs of reading each other's minds, understanding your spouse when their words don't make sense and ministering to their needs as they arise. It's here that the process of becoming one flesh is actually happening. This process of becoming one flesh is not easy. Becoming one flesh not only happens over decades but during this process, it's painful. Yelling, silence, long talks, sleeping on the sofa, not feeling understood or appreciated are all a part of it. These moments are manifestations of the progressive miracle we call marriage.

If you have raised a child or teenager you expect conflict, disagreements, anger, uprisings, repenting and many other sorts of painful experiences. These processes tell you they are alive and growing. How you handle these conflicts is important in parenting as well as in the miracle of your marriage.

You must, however accept the fact that all human relationships are painful, whether it is the child-parent, student-teacher, employee-employer, brother-sister, friend-friend or husband-wife relationship. In every relationship there is guaranteed pain.

The idea of pain being a guarantee in any relationship can bring comfort. Pain is a sign that something is alive and it needs attention. Pain is normal and healthy in a marriage. If we know it's guaranteed to come, it will be easier to process when it does.

When you go to the dentist or doctor's office and they pull out a huge needle, they may take a moment to explain why this cold, steel pointed needle needs to go painfully into your body. As they're talking to you, it's apparent you need to prepare for pain. Here's a secret I think every couple should know in premarital counseling, pain is coming. Pain doesn't mean you married the wrong person; you get to experience pain no matter who you are.

So if you are in a painful day or season of your marriage, your marriage is alive. Becoming one flesh is painful by design. So when it's happening, rejoice! "Rejoice?" you may ask. Yes, rejoice. It's in my personal and clinical experience of more than twenty years that after those painful events one or both of you mature and actually feel closer to each other. This is the warm and fuzzy feeling after someone dies a little bit more to themself, and it's awesome.

Another characteristic of becoming one flesh is conflict. You will inevitably have conflict. This conflict is also a precursor to change and growth toward becoming one flesh. This conflict is a part of your miracle progressing toward becoming a fully functioning trinity.

When you have two universes of ideas, experiences, agendas and genders, you will have conflict. Conflict must occur to expose what is in your heart or mind. Exposing flesh with truth or opposing ideas can bring a wobbling two headed creature into agreement. Conflict is healthy for your marriage so that it can grow stronger.

Conflict is not always huge and about money or sex. Conflict is also the small things in a marriage like how you fold socks and other insignificant things that move you into full engagement.

I want to share with you a brilliant principle God gave to Lisa and me very early in our marriage which reduced a significant amount of potential conflicts over the twenty-five years we have been married. Here is the principle, "If I am doing it, I am doing it right. If you criticize me, you get to do it."

So here is how this principle works practically. Let's go back to the major disagreement of folding socks. Lisa likes to ball up the socks when she folds laundry. I like my socks just folded not balled up like a dog toy. So if Lisa is folding laundry and I complain, she can ask me (politely of course) if I would like to fold all the laundry. If I continue to complain even one word after that, I get to fold the laundry. Likewise if I am folding the socks (not balling them up like a dog toy) and she complains, after me asking her if she wants to fold all the laundry, she would get to do this.

This is great for Lisa and me. We are both competent adults. We are both really good problem solvers, so we respect each other. There is usually three ways to do something, so if my way isn't right and hers is wrong, it's just her way and if I prefer it different, I need to put my life energy into doing it, not ask her to conform to my way of doing things.

Conflict will be a part of becoming one flesh. When you have conflict I would encourage you to follow a few principles to make it as smooth as possible.

Stay focused on one problem at a time. A spouse that moves to several problems to confuse their opponent rarely effectively solves problems. If you're arguing about socks, stay only on socks, don't bring dishes, their childhood, interest rates or something that happened three years ago into it. Couples who fight like that get more angry, use blame and take longer to reconnect. Honestly, it feels like a war zone when a couple does this in my office.

Secondly, before you solve a problem, make sure you hear each other's heart. This means discuss the feelings you have about the problem. Even around something as small as socks can make someone feel disrespected, unheard, unimportant, or misunderstood. Finding the feelings is part of hearing the heart of the other person. This can save you hours of arguing if you can hear one another's heart.

A second aspect of hearing the heart is trying to identify any symbolism of the event or anything you're in conflict about. Men can have symbols, however my experience is women tend to have more symbols in their communication. If the man doesn't know he is dealing with a symbol, he is handicapped in the conversation and frustrated. She is also frustrated, because he doesn't understand the symbol.

For example, on Mother's day, your father-in-law always bought a corsage for his wife. In their family the corsage became a symbol of honoring the wife for being a mother. Your wife as a little girl recognized this as a symbol. corsage equals honoring a woman for being a mom. You usually buy the corsage on Mother's Day, but this particular year you forgot. Your wife is really upset and you are clueless; after all, in your mind it's just a flower.

A corsage, my male friend, is a symbol of honoring your wife and you just dishonored her. So ask your wife if this is a symbol and have her explain it to you. Can I give wives a tip here as well?

Your husband is absolutely clueless to symbols and their hidden or deeper meanings. When you don't disclose the symbol he feels like you are playing a cruel game with him that he can't win. I get symbols only because I have counseled women for more than twenty years, but symbols are not always rational, and if they are not disclosed they will exasperate a conflict significantly. It can be that you aren't aware yourself of the symbol. While this is possible, it is also possible you know it's a symbol, so disclose it so your husband has an opportunity to understand you better, even if you think it makes little sense.

I'll never forget after a fairly significant conflict in our early marriage, Lisa disclosed a symbol to me. It's a long story how we come from two different garbage universes, but the bottom line is that Lisa disclosed that taking out the garbage really means (this is a symbol) that I love her. Once I knew that, as crazy as it sounds, I took out the garbage for many years. Now she feels loved even if she takes the garbage out (symbols change and disappear). So if there is a symbol, try to discover this to make your conflicts less painful.

Another suggestion about conflict I would give you both is to find the buttons. When in conflict, if your spouse is giving you Level 20 response, for a Level

2 response, you have found a button. Buttons unlike symbols usually make sense.

A man gets loud and the wife gets really scared, or even shuts down. When you understand she was regularly physically abused after her dad escalated, this button makes sense. I will never forget a particular guy in my office. Every time his wife made a request, his body got tight and he would say you're not going to control me. His mother viciously controlled him as a child and teenager, so a button was pushed when his wife would suggest things to him.

In conflict, when a button is pushed, that person may be too irrational to process the button at that moment because they are responding from their past not their present. You might want to exit this conflict right away, "We're getting too upset right now, let's address this in an hour or tomorrow." When the person is calm, ask about earlier times they felt like this or what situation in their childhood this reminds them of.

Identifying a button can save a lot of wear and tear in your marriage. If the button continues, seek out a counselor to heal that hurt so it doesn't infect the marriage during conflict. Conflict is challenging enough without buttons.

Lastly, brainstorm. When you get to the solution side of a conflict, "What three ideas do you have to solve this problem?" is a great question. This question gets you to utilize your creativity and a larger portion of your brain to solve a problem as opposed to your first idea and bullying your spouse to submit to what may not be the best idea at all. Having three solutions gives you both the confidence that at least some thought went into truly solving the problem.

> *God created you both to solve problems and if you're still stuck or better yet, before you get to that point of getting stuck, stop and pray for God to reveal some solutions.*

Remember, the problem is the problem and people are the solution. God created you both to solve problems and if you're still stuck or better yet, before you get to that point of getting stuck, stop and pray for God to reveal some solutions. Honestly, some of the best solutions were when Lisa and I prayed about it and the next day, after a good night's sleep, the solution became obvious to us both and some of the previous ideas in hindsight were not the best decisions.

Conflict will always be with you, however if the goal is to become one flesh, you will want to capitalize on conflict to move you toward agreement and resolve so that you both now think as one on another issue. Now let's hold hands and walk through this process of the miracle of marriage. I do this so you can see the journey of God walking with you in your miracle process.

Your miracle of marriage started way before your wedding day. Just like a sonogram, the miracle of life, a child, occurs way before birth. It's that moment or series of moments, when you are realizing that this is a special person to you. It seems undeniable. You ache for them. When you are with them, there is a love and respect for each other. You work through some issues that bond you further together and you know that you know, they are the one for you. Your miracle was conceived here, surrounded by warmth and love, respect, quality communication, quality time, and positive reinforcement from your peers and/or family over time.

Then there is a pulsing as your miracle of marriage moves more toward its third trimester. You get engaged and now the third trimester is in full swing. The stresses of the upcoming marriage expose some ideas or relationships that raise questions. Your future marriage is having to solve problems and is not just entertaining one another. Family loyalties are challenged and painting a picture of your wedding and honeymoon together exposes your early negotiation conflict styles and tools, roles or the lack of any of these in your life. Your maturity or immaturity is also challenged in this third and final trimester of a developing marriage.

The day comes when you arise early for the big day, dressing in outfits that are totally amazing. You look and feel better than any other day in your life.

She walks down the aisle like an angel, you say the vows, till death do you part, kiss each other and it's official-your miracle of marriage is birthed.

Now your miracle of marriage is officially an infant. In this stage, like a baby, you both need to focus on the immediate needs of survival. You have immediate needs for food, shelter, cars and jobs. In this stage, you are learning new things about your spouse at a rapid rate including their eating, sleeping, and relationship habits. You are navigating sexual appetites and boundaries as a new born marriage as well. You are also fettering through both spouse's friends determining who is good for the marriage. You may still have some of your previous habits such as dating, quality time, talks and infatuation and gratitude for your spouse.

The marriage continues to grow year after year. You may buy a new car, a house, start to invest money, establish a church family, and hopefully tithe. Your marriage in this toddler stage is stabilized financially, relationally, vocationally, and spiritually as it starts to take roots. In this stage of marriage, you have established the bigger boundaries and try to be reasonable in your marriage as you both are maturing, barring any serious addictions or personality disorders.

For many couples it happens to them at this point. They feel stable, are in love with each other and want to start having children. She gets pregnant and now the marriage is in the elementary years of its life. Pregnancy demands that both spouses mature even more. She has more needs now along with doctor's appointments, and he gets concerned about her, as well as how to provide for his future family.

This elementary stage is critical before your marriage goes to the next stage. In this stage, your values can change significantly. You start a whole new series of negotiating family type issues, along with new conflicts and clarifications occur as you, as a couple with God, become one flesh for this child.

The child is born and you are officially parents. There is not enough preparation for this junior high stage of your marriage. You figure out some of the earlier roles, how to live without as much sleep, spending more money or time and as the child matures, both of you become more selfless. You grow a lot in the junior high stage of marriage especially as you have multiple children.

Now your marriage's high school stage begins as children continue to grow through their toddler, pre-school, elementary and junior high school years. Their growth through these stages continues to clarify your values as a couple. Hopefully, during this stage of your marriage, you are still dating each other, are attending a local church and have some friendships as you create an environment for your children to prosper.

Then your marriage goes to college as your children go through high school. Adolescents require a significantly different set of tactics for the marriage to do well. Your children now have abstract reasoning and sexuality to manage at the same time. Giving your adolescent child wings and teaching them how to make decisions is different than having them obey you. Your marriage will have further value clarifications and conflicts as the three of you: God, husband, and wife become one in order to begin to launch these children into their own faith, their giftedness and preparing them for the following stages of independence from you.

As they leave, one by one, you realize, "You did it!" They have moved out of your house and are starting a life, career, and relationships independent of you. You, as empty nesters, are now in the young adult stage of your marriage.

This is a very critical point of a marriage. If you have abandoned each other during the parenting years a new commitment to the spouse will be necessary as you deal with this stage of marriage. Often in this stage of marriage your level of financial preparation and marital preparation will start paying off in freedom, or your lack of preparedness for the future will be an issue to address.

In this stage, you can have more time together, re-explore and re-clarify goals for your marriage, recapture romance, have a healthy dating and sex life and breathe a little. Your marriage often stabilizes for a period of time in this young adult stage of marriage. In this stage, your children often get married as well and start their journey of life.

A new person may be added to your marriage here. This time the baby you're holding in the delivery room isn't yours, it's your children's child; your grandbaby. They tell me all grandbabies are perfect and it's at this time your marriage moves into its midlife stage.

You hopefully still have good health; one or both of you may be toward the end of a career or are starting retirement. You are aware of your financial needs and adjust accordingly. You have friends and hopefully some hobbies or ministry you're involved with. This season also has you clarify values and is often a stable season of a marriage in many respects.

Here your marriage begins to enter its final stage, that of a senior marriage. This stage will have its challenges with possibly health, finance and family issues. However, if a couple remains intimate and prayerful, they can drink from the sweetness of both becoming more Christ like through all the stages of marriage. If you did not let this miracle of marriage allow you to become Christ like, this stage of marriage will truly be a challenge.

Eventually, death temporarily takes one of you. My hope is that I get to be married to Lisa in that thousand year reign with Christ on the earth and live close by her in heaven since she is my best friend in the world.

I hope you enjoyed this panoramic view of your miracle. I realize everyone doesn't have these exact steps and that tragedies can alter your life. However, I do think overall it's largely helpful to see the movie of your marriage rather than just a photograph. Some photographs in a marriage can be of not the best moments, but the overall movie can be tremendous. This miracle of your marriage is progressive and the miracle of God walking through each stage is truly the sweetest part of your marriage journey.

The theme of this movie is God walking with you and your spouse on a unique journey to reveal Himself and to make you one. Your unique movie is amazing with an amazing God who makes each scene its absolute best for others to behold His story through you.

Your marriage is a testimony so that the lost and the saved can say, "I see God here and here..." "Look how they climbed out of that or avoided this." Your marriage is a progressive story and you both play a significant part in giving God glory as you progress through this miracle called marriage.

God has called each one of us,

men and women,

to care for the garden

He has chosen to give us.

Maintaining the Miracle 5

Let's go back to the Garden of Eden to show you an amazing fact as it relates to the creation of man. Afterward we will then transport into the New Testament and expand on this idea to show you a principle that if you both buy into fully, will optimize your miracle of marriage.

> "... and there was no one to work the ground,"
>
> Genesis 2:5

Let's go back to Genesis 2:5 where it says that God has not sent rain on the earth and, "there was no man to work the ground." It appears that God was making all of creation and was looking for man to work it, maintain it, and care for this amazing creation.

> "The Lord took the man and put him in the Garden of Eden to work it and take care of it."
> Genesis 2:15

Genesis 2:15 confirms this idea of man's commission to maintain and care for this creation. "The Lord took the man and put him in the Garden of Eden to work it and take care of it."

Often when I am sharing this in a marriage conference, I'll say to the men that all of us are simply maintenance men. God has called each one of us, men and women, to care for the garden He has chosen to give us.

Let me continue to talk to the men for a moment. Men, everything in your garden is yours to maintain. Everything and everyone in your garden requires maintenance. This maintenance must come only from you. Only you can maintain the people and things God gives to you in your garden. When I accept this, that it's my responsibility before God to maintain or care for my garden, it helps me to not be resistant towards doing the dishes, laundry, or big projects around the house. Maintaining the garden is the first calling of all of ours.

Remember that this calling to maintain the garden preceded the law or sin. Adam and Eve's calling to maintain comes out of God's design for them, even in a sinless world. The calling to maintain is not a result of the fall. The fall made maintaining more difficult and challenging. The fall added pain to a process that was probably a lot easier before the fall.

To maintain is to be in alignment with you being created in the image of God. To maintain a woman or maintain a man is a calling of God in which he has uniquely equipped you to do. Now in our sin nature we can resist this calling and the blessing of walking in this calling, but it is a calling and responsibility given by God to both of you.

It is totally awesome to me that I am in the center of God's will when I am maintaining. I personally get pleasure out of washing a car, picking up and putting things away again, because I know God is pleased when I maintain the garden. This paradigm of maintaining man on assignment from God makes some of the less than fun tasks more palatable.

It reminds me of a scene from a movie I saw called "Blues Brothers" before I was saved. The character played by John Bellushi said he "...was on a mission from God." As men and women, we are on a maintenance mission from God.

Also I have to remind men that Eve was in the garden too. She also is part of that responsibility to maintain and care for the garden. Eve needs to be maintained by Adam. Eve, Adam is in your garden and yes, he has some needs only you can maintain and that is the blessing of God in marriage to maintain each other.

Maintaining isn't a popular idea here in the United States. We like to hire someone to do this or that for us. We don't even wash our cars anymore; we let a machine do this for us called a car wash. In a culture that is moving further and further from the reality of maintenance, we can lose the very fabric that life is maintenance.

The fact that all of life is maintenance can be felt as painful or delightful to you. I enjoy having a house and that house requires maintenance every change of season. I also have a car and it requires maintenance. If I maintain it well, it is more likely to serve me better and longer over the years. However, if maintenance is a burden or painful, you can employ a technique I have seen many addicts employ in their life called denial. You can simply deny life or that your spouse needs maintenance and then have those things break down more often and require even more maintenance later on. Let me tell you a story I tell the men in the "How to Really Love a Woman" conferences.

As a Christian guy you're driving down the freeway. You're coming down a hill and you see smoke coming from under the hood of a car that is pulled over on the side of the road a mile or more away. As you get closer it's this year's model of Lamborghini. Being the good Christian that you are (and you want a better look at this very expensive car) you want to help, so you pull over.

A twenty something year old young man comes out of the car. You're wondering whether this is a very bright fellow or a trust fund kid. You politely ask this young man what's wrong with the car. He tells you the engine is locked up. You ask, when did you last have your oil changed?

The young man says that he doesn't believe in oil changes (maintenance), he thinks it's some government scam or something incoherent like that. Now you're thinking this is definitely a trust fund kid!

Everyone knows to change the oil in the car. You know that a locked up engine is a result of neglecting the maintenance over a long period of time (denial of maintenance). You and I know it's so much cheaper to pay for consistent oil changes than it is to fix or replace a seized engine.

Marriage is just like that as well, it is cheaper to apply a few principles consistently to maintain your marriage than it is to neglect the God given maintenance in a marriage. If it locks up due to denial of the maintenance principle you end up spending so much more on a professional counselor or worse on divorce attorneys.

Let's look at the word of God to validate that marriage is maintenance of a special kind indeed. Turn in your Bible to Ephesians 5:25-31. As I write this, I know that often the author pens the large idea on a subject then gives the how to's or more practical steps following the large idea.

> "Husbands, love your wives, just as Christ loved the church and gave Himself up for her to make her holy, cleansing her by the washing with water through the Word and to present her to himself as a radiant church, without stain or wrinkle or any other blemish, but holy and blameless. Husbands ought to love their wives as their own bodies. He who loves his wife loves himself, after all, no one ever hated his own body, but feeds and cares for it just as Christ does the church for we are members of his body. For this reason a man will leave his father and mother and be united to his wife, and the two will become one flesh."
> Ephesians 5:25-31

Paul, the author of Ephesians, follows the path of the large idea first followed by the how to's. He states in this section with the big idea of "Husbands, love your wives, just as Christ loved the church and gave Himself up for her to make her holy, cleansing her by the washing with water through the Word (27) and to present her to himself as a radiant church, without stain or wrinkle or any other blemish, but holy and blameless."

I must say this is a really large idea. Guys, love your wife like Jesus. I have spoken at so many marriage conferences and this verse never gets an "amen" (at least by a man) no matter where I read it. I think we feel like a failure when we compare our selfish selves as a husband to Jesus. However, that's the large idea and when you understand the how to's, it's relatively easy to feel confident when this scripture is read.

Paul then moves on to the "how to" section of this scripture. He starts with a great phrase, "In this same way" in other words, just like this and you could get the way to actually do what he is talking about in regards to loving your wife.

Paul continues, "Husbands ought to love their wives as their own bodies. He who loves his wife loves himself (29) after all, no one ever hated his own body, but feeds and cares for it just as Christ does the church (30) for we are members of his body (31). For this reason a man will leave his father and mother and be united to his wife, and the two will become one flesh" the final creation of God, His masterpiece, a marriage.

I want us to really understand what is being said here. Paul suggests that taking care of a wife (or a spouse for that matter) is like feeding and caring for your body both in fact and in attitude.

Factually, let's go through your feeding and caring for

your physical body. Let's talk about food. Firstly, you work for food, then shop for it, then cook it, then eat it, then clean up afterward, and then put the dishes away after the dishwasher does the hard work of washing the dishes. I think on average it would be very safe to say each of us spends a minimum of two hours a day just feeding our body.

Then let's talk about that bath, shower, drying the hair, getting dressed routine you go through every day of your life. I think most of us donate a half hour to an hour a day just to wash our body.

Another step in caring for your body is sleep. For most of us, sleep is a six to eight hour investment of caring for our bodies. You can see that caring for yourself on a daily basis is time consuming even on the short ride of 2 hours to eat, 30 minutes to shower and six hour to sleep. This low maintenance is factually committing a minimum of eight hours and thirty minutes a day to self care. That is one third of your day committed to the caring and feeding of your body. That doesn't include exercise, doctor, dentist or eye doctor appointments and that's if you are healthy.

Attitude is a very important aspect of maintenance. How many of you before you eat a great meal, curse God? "God, why do I have to work to eat, cook and clean up? Why have you cursed me with this maintenance?" How about in the shower as you get cleansed and smell great by all the products you have in that shower, do you curse God? "God, why do I have to spend all this time in the shower, and the cost of soap...?"

How about sleep? You're tired, so you go to sleep, get a good rest. Do you wake up and curse God? "God, why do I have to sleep? What a waste of time." I hope none of us is so ungrateful for our daily bread, shower and sleep. I bless God for these gifts of maintenance. I really enjoy a good meal, a good shower, and great sleep. I feel especially blessed if I get all three on a regular basis like you and I so often do in this country.

At a very core level, you fully accept with gratitude the DAILY maintenance of your body. In this same way, when you at the core of your heart fully accept the daily maintenance of your wife or husband you will be happy to maintain them on a daily basis.

Christ doesn't show up and feed His church irregularly, but daily. If you, as an individual, accept fully that marriage is a daily discipline, marriage can be so much easier. Until you fully accept the daily maintenance of your spouse, you may be angry about it, bargain about it, be sad about it, or even just deny their need for daily maintenance by you, and you alone.

This principle can really set you free, depending upon your response to the very real reality that your spouse requires daily maintenance. If you accept this maintenance principle you have a grateful attitude. Just like you thank God for the food, shower or sleep, you thank God for the spouse and your calling to maintain them.

If, however, you have hardened your heart, the daily maintenance of this child of God will be a burden. You will be burdened by praying with them, sharing your heart, dating, sex, as well as the emotional, and financial cost of a spouse. Maintenance exposes our hearts. If we do this cheerfully, then I think we understand what Jesus feels when He serves His church every day.

I love the conclusion of Paul's thoughts here, especially in the light of marriage being God's final creation. He states, "For this reason a man will leave his father and mother and be united to his wife."

We all go through the process of being maintained by our parents, and learning how to maintain ourselves so we can learn how to daily maintain our spouse, this is a brilliant process. Then Paul continues, quoting this scripture from the book of Genesis, "And the two will become one flesh."

If we accept our full responsibility to maintain our spouse this process leads us into the glorious creation of a Godly marriage on earth. When you have a heart of grateful maintenance, you will just try to meet the needs of your spouse's heart, body, sexuality, financially, and parenting, without judging their validity against your own preconceived grid. In the beginning of this chapter we laid down the idea that we are all called to maintain our garden. God has placed your spouse in your garden. You fully accept your daily maintenance without a negative attitude.

To be Christ like is to accept the maintenance of your spouse with a good attitude.

This really is glorious and excites me so much that I am going to get up right now and get some dishes done before my wife comes home. If you get the ideas in this chapter, you might also have some creative ideas on how to maintain your spouse.

I think it's incumbent upon us to ask ourselves, be a husband or a wife, "What kind of maintenance person am I toward my spouse?" If Jesus was giving me a grade today on how well I have been maintaining my spouse, what grade would He give me?

Regardless of your answers to these questions you have today and the rest of your life to be the most awesome maintenance of your spouse. I say go for the gold when it comes to maintaining your spouse.

Miracles,
especially the miracle of
your marriage,
needs to be protected.

Protecting the Miracle 6

Every once in a while a corporation gets a tag line to promote their business that becomes part of American culture. I think of Nike "Just Do It" and Chick-fil-A' "Eat Mor Chikin" a sign held up by a couple of cows. Recently I was in a sporting goods store and I saw the tag line for Under Armor, a sportswear line and I loved it. The tag line simply said, "Protect This House."

As a man, of course that tag line speaks to the most primitive part of me as a protector. Miracles, especially the miracle of your marriage, needs to be protected. Let's go back to the baby analogy that we have spent time on previously.

That little infant, toddler, child, and adolescent needs to be protected. We don't put our infant on the floor in a public place where it could risk being injured, rather we hold it, protect it until it can incrementally protect itself. There also is a need to protect your marriage, no matter how old the marriage.

There are three broad ideas that can be helpful for you to consider as you desire to protect your marriage. The first category of this discussion is what I simply call "bad ideas."

Bad Ideas

Lying

When someone believes that they can start lying to

their spouse, it instantly creates problems in the marriage. Lying is totally counterproductive to the design of God in this creation we call marriage. Remember, God's admiration of His final creation, this miracle of marriage, is that they be naked and feel no shame.

One thing I know about lying after working with couples for more than twenty years, there is absolutely no upside. Firstly, lying denies the presence and person of God. To lie is to say God, you didn't see that. God you don't care that I lie, and God I am not accountable to you. So lying disturbs your perception of who God really is.

Secondly, lying creates a wall between you and your spouse that is definitely felt. There is something going on between the two of you even if it is as simple as you're angry at yourself for lying and you eventually take your anger out on yourself or on your spouse.

Thirdly, this is for the guys because women will already, at least intuitively, understand these two ideas. Your wife absolutely has no way to process a lie. When you choose to lie to your wife she feels disrespected and hurt because you didn't trust her enough to give her the truth. It's like saying to her, "I don't trust you and I don't care." You are rejecting your wife's person when you lie to her and create intentional pain in your marriage. So guys, if you want to do something your wife won't understand and is guaranteed to be hurt in your marriage, lie.

I'm sure some guys are thinking that the information would hurt their wife and that you are trying to protect her. That is simply not true. Ask your wife if she wants you to lie to her and see what she says. In almost every case, the husband made a major or minor mistake and doesn't want to look bad, flawed, or just plain stupid and so he covers up by lying to his wife. In my book, that is cowardly. What I have learned about manhood is basic. I will make mistakes, and when I do, I'll admit them fully to my wife, my accountability people, the person I hurt, and I'll take the consequence fully. A boy tries to cover up, lie, manipulate, and blame when he does something less than wonderful. I didn't say "if" he does something less than wonderful but WHEN. I'm a guy. I absolutely know I make mistakes. The beauty of it is if I choose honesty, I grow toward my spouse and absorb wisdom so I don't keep doing that same mistake. If not, I create distance and usually make bigger mistakes so that I can gain the gift of humility. This is the same humility I could have gained from the smaller mistake had I been honest.

Let me be totally clear here to both of you. There is no such thing as a secret.

Let me be totally clear here to both of you. There is no such thing as a secret. I have counseled couples for more than two decades and some have lied so often to their spouse that they needed to utilize a polygraph service in our office just to stop lying and rebuild trust. You can avoid this path toward the destruction of this living creation of God's, your marriage, simply by practicing honesty.

Low Priority

Over the years I have seen several causes for a marriage to get to a crisis level. In some instances, it's not about the big fights over money, children, or even the extra marital relationships. There is a bad idea that can, long-term, make a marriage vulnerable to a crisis and even cause a divorce. This bad idea I call "low priority" because one or both people in the marriage do not consider their marriage valuable enough to intentionally keep working on it, day in and day out, or with any type of plan.

Often this couple gets distracted by their developmental tasks of money, shelter, children, planning for the future, and loses sight of the true miracle of their marriage. They tend to try to get along, have cyclical friction and just plow through. Intimacy, at an emotional level, is accidental or a result of the last crisis.

These are usually good people, but with no plan. This is similar to the good people who didn't plan on retirement throughout their marriage and ended up depending on social security. It's better to have a plan to stay connected (which I'll talk more about in the chapter on Principles for a Miracle) throughout the lifespan of your marriage, than to just default to "whatever". Whatever may work for a while but when it's a regularly traveled road then it usually ends up in my office and other counselors' offices throughout the country.

Let me give you a good example of purposeful intention from a pastor friend of mine who I really respect. He has a clear plan to maintain his marriage. Every year he and his wife get a couple of marriage counseling sessions with one of the counselors in my office. These appointments cover the structures in their marriage as well as issues that have come up for them as a couple. He wants someone speaking health into his marriage before it gets clogged up or dysfunctional

Also this pastor attends one marriage conference a year. I know because he sat in a couple of my conferences over the years. He and his wife are intentional. They have committed to a couple of principles to actively make their marriage a priority. This pastor can easily suggest these proactive approaches to his congregation becuuse he and his wife personally do them. I wish all of our spiritual leaders were as focused on maintaining a good marriage.

Entertainment

This bad idea, entertainment, is probably the sneakiest of them all. I am not against any couple having some entertainment in their life. However, I have seen entertainment become such a time consumer of so many couples that I have to discuss it in this section of bad ideas.

Firstly, most of you reading this book are among the richest people in the world. I don't mean you are Bill Gates or Warren Buffet. However you all do live in a house or apartment, have a microwave, refrigerator, dishwasher, and television and more than enough food and still have discretionary income. You are rich by any global standard. So most of you are not experiencing life so hard that you need to escape by being entertained for hours a day, or twenty to forty hours a week.

Sadly though, most couples have never even honestly addressed how much entertainment is reasonable. Again, this is much like the couple who never decides how much money to save. One couple can end up financially having regrets and the other can have regrets how they invested their one life on planet earth sitting in front of a screen.

Before we go further into this discussion, let's look at the various categories of entertainment you can have in your life.

- Television
- Internet
- Virtual communities
- Videogames/Internet gaming
- Newspaper
- Books

- Music
- Catalogs
- Movies
- Hobbies
- Sports playing
- Magazines
- Theater
- DVDs
- Sports watching
- Other

There are so many forms of entertaining yourself these days. Again, I'm not against some entertainment but so many couples major in entertainment and actually minor in their marriage or ministry to others in their community because they are so busy investing in entertainment.

Before we take one more step down the road of entertainment, I want you to try a little exercise. On the following chart you will see again a list of these areas of entertainment. I want you to write down how much time you each spend individually and as a couple on each form of entertainment.

Weekly Entertainment Time

Activity	His Time	Her Time	Together Time
Television			
Internet			
Virtual communities			
Video games/ Internet gaming			
Newspaper			
Books			
Music			
Magazines			

Activity	His Time	Her Time	Together Time
Catalogs			
Theater			
Movies			
DVDs			
Hobbies			
Sports watching			
Sports playing			
Other			
Total			

How much time do you currently spend on entertainment as a couple in a week? Think about this time. Is it too little, too much, just about right? What do you really think about investing your limited quantity of time in this manner? Better yet, take a moment and together ask the third person in this triune miracle marriage, your Heavenly Father, what He thinks about this time commitment and investment in entertainment.

Entertainment has so many ways to creep into a marriage. If your marriage is really strong and you have more hours spent on entertainment, than might be acceptable here and there. This would be like the couple who mostly saves their money, but occasionally spends more. They still will be stable financially. However, the couple who overspends regularly will be in trouble long-term. The couple who over entertains will also have difficulty long-term.

I've had couples tell me I didn't understand that they were bored. To that I say go witness to people, pray for the sick, or get involved somewhere to help others. That eliminates boredom instantly.

One other issue for couples is the type of entertainment they participate in. I put entertainment into three camps. The first camp is Godly entertainment. This entertainment clearly promotes Godly ideas and values. The second is a neutral camp. This entertainment doesn't really clash with God's values; it may promote secular or worldly ideas. The third camp of entertainment clearly promotes secular or ungodly beliefs and behaviors that are contrary to God's ways and heart. An example of a TV show that promotes cheating on your spouse would be the third camp of entertainment.

Now let's do one more exercise on entertainment. Remember the list you made that clarified your time spent on entertainment? Now I want you to clarify the percentage of each form of entertainment into those three categories, Godly (G), Neutral (N), Secular (S).

Entertainment Categories Chart

Activity	His			Her		
Television	G___%	N___%	S___%	G___%	N___%	S___%
Internet	G___%	N___%	S___%	G___%	N___%	S___%
Virtual communities	G___%	N___%	S___%	G___%	N___%	S___%
Video/Internet gaming	G___%	N___%	S___%	G___%	N___%	S___%
Newspaper	G___%	N___%	S___%	G___%	N___%	S___%
Books	G___%	N___%	S___%	G___%	N___%	S___%
Music	G___%	N___%	S___%	G___%	N___%	S___%
Magazines	G___%	N___%	S___%	G___%	N___%	S___%
Catalogs	G___%	N___%	S___%	G___%	N___%	S___%
Theater	G___%	N___%	S___%	G___%	N___%	S___%
Movies	G___%	N___%	S___%	G___%	N___%	S___%

Activity	His	Her
DVDs	G___% N___% S___%	G___% N___% S___%
Hobbies	G___% N___% S___%	G___% N___% S___%
Sports watching	G___% N___% S___%	G___% N___% S___%
Sports playing	G___% N___% S___%	G___% N___% S___%
Other	G___% N___% S___%	G___% N___% S___%

As you did this exercise, I hope you gained insight. Which category of entertainment do you mostly consume on a regular basis and why? Which entertainment do you consume the least and why? Is your consumption of secular or ungodly entertainment at a level you agree with?

Everybody has heard the saying, you are what you eat. I believe this applies to entertainment as well. If you marinate in Godly ideas, you are more likely to produce Godly behavior. If you marinate in ungodly ideas of lust, lying, disrespect, and materialism, you will be more susceptible to these beliefs and will be manifesting these behaviors in your life. Remember Lot vexed (tortured) his soul just by hearing and seeing unrighteousness. Just watching bad stuff can affect the condition of your soul which could impact your marriage.

You deserve the best miracle of marriage you can have. Evaluating entertainment is an important part of having a healthy marriage. Just like the couple who doesn't plan to save inherits poverty so it is with a couple who over invests in entertainment. They will have poverty in some area of their life.

If you are a couple whose entertainment is out of balance, I have a great idea. As a couple, create a media budget. Decide intentionally how much time a week you dedicate and commit to be entertained. You decide, 5 hours, 10 hours, 20, 30 hours a week, and then stick to your budget. If you stay inside your budget, you can give yourself a reward. If you find yourself over-entertained, then get accountable to another couple or set some consequences or better yet do both, to be as successful as you can.

Pornography

I would be remiss if I didn't talk about this subject under protecting your marriage. I have seen the total devastation that stems from pornography and inappropriate behaviors. I have written several books on sexual addiction and its impact on the spouse and children.

Some have suggested that 50% of the men in the church are sexually addicted. When I speak at men's conferences I have them close their eyes and well over 50% will identify with being currently sexually addicted.

Many Christian women are in absolute denial that this could ever be happening in their marriage. Ladies, as a way to protect your marriage, I suggest you move from a policy of "don't ask, don't tell" to a policy of "trust but verify." Ladies, you are the ones who are at risk with his infidelity, STD's, being a single mother, or retiring alone due to his behavior. James 1:15, "Then, after desire has conceived, it gives birth to sin; and sin, when it is full-grown, gives birth to death," is clear about the progression of lust, sin and death in a person's life. You deserve to have this destroyed in your marriage. Ladies, I am strongly suggesting you ask your husband several times a year these two questions:

1. When was the last time you looked at pornography?
2. When was the last time you masturbated?

I could fill a room with the tears good Christian

women who never asked, and are now dealing with a damaged marriage and a family at risk. When I asked these wives if they directly asked their husband, they always say no. I understand they didn't know to ask, but now you know to ask directly.

Men, if you are struggling here, get honest and the sooner the better. Get accountable and free. Most men and women who struggle with pornography stay sick because they protect the secret. James 5:16, "Therefore confess your sins to each other and pray for each other so that you may be healed. The prayer of a righteous person is powerful and effective" says if we confess our sins to one another we can be healed. Confessing just to Jesus gets you forgiven. 1 John 1:9, "If we confess our sins, he is faithful and just and will forgive us our sins and purify us from all unrighteousness," confessing to another person gets you healed. You can be forgiven and not healed.

Here are a few other ideas to help protect your marriage from pornography.

- Go to our website www.drdougweiss.com and get a porn blocker on all your computers.

- You can also add an accountability feature that emails you reports as to each website visited.

- Block the Internet from your spouse's cell phone.

- Block or control any cable television.

- Have same sex accountability.

- If addicted, do a free assessment by phone by calling Heart to Heart Counseling Center at 719-278-3708

- If addicted join a local or phone Freedom Group,

- If you're a spouse of an addict, also get helpful materials and get in a group,

- You can do phone sessions or 3 Day Intensives as well.

Pornography is a real killer of Christian marriages today. There is another side effect to someone that struggles with pornography that can also choke a marriage to death. We call it intimacy anorexia and about one third of sexually addicted men and their spouses have this relationship pattern. Intimacy anorexia is the active withholding of spiritual, emotional and sexual intimacy. Some anorexics don't withhold sexually but are not present during sex either.

Below are the characteristics of an intimacy anorexic. If you answer 5 or more of these characteristics I would strongly recommend our DVD, book and workbooks on "Intimacy Anorexia" and "Married and

Alone" sets to start your healing process, as well as phone counseling, or 3 Day Intensives.

Intimacy Anorexia

For Him

	Yes	No
Staying so busy that you have little time for your spouse	___	___
When issues come up, your first reflex or response is to blame your spouse	___	___
Withholding love from your spouse	___	___
Withholding praise from your spouse	___	___
Withholding sex from your spouse or not being present during sex	___	___
Withholding spiritual connection from your spouse	___	___
Unwilling or unable to share your authentic feelings with your spouse	___	___
Using anger or silence to control your spouse	___	___

Having ongoing or ungrounded criticism (spoken or unspoken) toward your spouse ____ ____
Controlling or shaming your spouse regarding money or spending ____ ____

For Her

Yes No

Staying so busy that you have little time for your spouse ____ ____
When issues come up, your first reflex or response is to blame your spouse ____ ____
Withholding love from your spouse ____ ____
Withholding praise from your spouse ____ ____
Withholding sex from your spouse or not being present during sex ____ ____
Withholding spiritual connection from your spouse ____ ____
Unwilling or unable to share your authentic feelings with your spouse ____ ____
Using anger or silence to control your spouse ____ ____

Having ongoing or ungrounded criticism
(spoken or unspoken) toward your spouse ___ ___
Controlling or shaming your spouse
regarding money or spending ___ ___

Others

The last area of protection I want to discuss is others. Protect your marriage from outside opposite sex relationships to lessen the chance of adultery. We live in a world where adultery is accepted and promoted. Christians who don't protect this area can be vulnerable to a tragic incident that can damage or destroy their marriage.

Here are some real quick tips to evaluate if you're protecting your marriage in this area.

1. Your spouse has access to your Facebook, email accounts, and cell phone.

2. No one-on-one time with the opposite sex without it being for professional purposes, even then your spouse should know about it.
3. If traveling, have a plan to be safe and accountable.
4. No opposite sex unprofessional texting or emailing.
5. Be honest about opposite sex conversations that are less than professional.
6. Never talk bad about your spouse to the opposite sex. This is a fishing expedition.
7. If you're not happy in your marriage, talk to your spouse or get professional help.
8. If sex is an issue, create a sexual agreement.

You absolutely deserve a great marriage. God wants you to have the best marriage but like many gifts of God, we must protect them. I hope these few ideas have helped you to better protect this miracle we call marriage.

I will briefly lay out several principles that when applied can help your marriage get and stay healthy.

Principles 7

Almost everything God creates has to be maintained as we discussed earlier. However, there are principles to maintaining a vehicle, a house, or a marriage. These principles exist regardless of your awareness or neglect of them.

Take, for example, your yard. If you have a sprinkler system, and live in an area where you actually receive the gift of winter, there is a principle to caring for your sprinkler system. Prior to winter you have all the water drained out of your sprinkler system. This is commonly called blowing out your system.

If you follow this principle of blowing out your system, you get a functional (healthy) sprinkler system the next spring. If however, you are ignorant of this principle, or you refuse to practice it, you will have the water freeze and break your sprinkler system to the point that it will have to be repaired or replaced. This would be the dysfunctional or unhealthy way to maintain your sprinkler system.

Let's utilize our ongoing analogy of children. There are definitely good principles in raising children. If you follow these principles you are more likely to have better results. In this case, you have the factor of free will. Even God's two children made mistakes. However, if you ignore these principles of parenting, or practice really toxic principles in parenting, you will have less of a chance of having successful children. Again, free will can change this. I know some awful parents whose children became successful in life because of the child's choice.

In this chapter, I will briefly lay out several principles that when applied can help your marriage get and stay healthy. I will be brief here. If you want more in depth information on these principles, I would refer you to the books Intimacy: A 100 Day Guide to Lasting Relationships (Siloam, 2003) or The Ten-Minute Marriage Principle: Quick, Daily Steps for Refreshing Your Relationship (Faith Words, 2007) or any of the many other good marriage books out there. These principles are not in any particular order, but they will assess your marriage in each area. They will be helpful for you to have conversations together about where you're doing well, and where you could utilize some adjusting in your miracle of marriage.

Spiritually Connected

As Christians, we have a very unique opportunity to be connected together to the one who has made both of us and our marriage. Couples who stay spiritually connected do so in several ways. Some couples pray together and I think this is a critical principle for a Christian marriage. Some couples read the Bible together. This can also be a great principle. I would add only one caution here, and that is to share what the Word is teaching you, and not what you think it should be teaching your spouse, as that can sour the reading of God's Word together.

Some couples worship together at home. They play a CD, DVD, play an instrument, or just sing together. This can be an awesome principle as well. Going to church is a great principle to do together. However, if your church attendance is similar to being entertained at a theater, this may be limiting its potential impact on your marriage. If you talk about the service and what you learned, it can be really helpful.

Serving in a church or ministry can also be a terrific way to stay spiritually connected. The experiences of ministry can be really bonding for the two of you to consistently stay connected. Regardless of how you stay spiritually connected, consistency is a very important principle for your miracle of marriage to stay strong over the decades.

How does he rate our spiritual connection?

Weak   Neutral   Strong   Very Strong

How does she rate our spiritual connection?

Weak   Neutral   Strong   Very Strong

Emotionally Connected

Staying emotionally connected is also critical for a high functioning, healthy marriage. I realize most of us have no emotional training. I have included a Feelings List in the Appendix. You can do this exercise to gain a tremendous emotional skill in your marriage. Couples that can trust their heart to their spouse can have amazing intimacy and fewer arguments. The couples that are walled off emotionally, have more significant hurdles in their relationships.

If you do the feelings exercise daily, it can increase your intimacy in weeks. You can also just randomly put feelings words in a jar and give examples about your life regarding the feeling picked. Anything you can do to talk about feelings can really help you have a healthy and more intimate marriage.

How does he rate our emotional connection?

Weak   *Neutral*   *Strong*   *Very Strong*

How does she rate our emotional connection?

Weak   *Neutral*   *Strong*   *Very Strong*

Stay Dating

The couples who date have created a principle that has several positive side effects. When a couple dates regularly (weekly or two times a month), they have created a timely escape valve from the pressures of life. A couple that has fun has more resources, because they recharge themselves so they can become more patient with each other and their family.

Dating also let's each of you remember why you wanted to get married. You begin to remember how witty, intelligent, and creative your spouse really is. I know just seeing Lisa smile makes the whole date worthwhile. Protecting your dating is important and it's really positive for the children if they are still home. Children feel more secure when parents want to be together. So date to keep your marriage healthy.

How does he rate our dating?

Weak   *Neutral*   *Strong*   *Very Strong*

How does she rate our dating?

Weak   *Neutral*   *Strong*   *Very Strong*

Finances

Often we bring much of what our family did or did not teach us into our marriage. Most couples will have one partner who is tighter and one that is looser in regards to spending. Tension builds between the present, and preparing for the future as well. The discipline of tithing, investing, saving, and living under your income are critical challenges for the marriage to stay financially healthy.

It's great for a couple to have a functional budget that reflects present realities and future goals. Money can be very emotional and maturity levels can get lowered quickly when somebody wants a toy.

This is one area, if it is not a strength, I say get help immediately. Most churches have a financial ministry of some type that can help with information and accountability. A couple who has this as a strength, worries less in the present and has hope for their future.

How does he rate our finances?

Weak   Neutral   Strong   Very Strong

How does she rate our finances?

Weak   Neutral   Strong   Very Strong

Parenting

This is by far the most challenging and emotionally charged subject for most couples that I have noticed in my practice. You have two genders, two worlds of experience, a varied and shifting value system, and that doesn't even bring into play the personalities of the children, and the personalities of the in-laws.

This is definitely an area where being in agreement as much as possible can be helpful. I really recommend that you read as much as possible for each developmental stage your children are experiencing. I recommend having mentors you trust to run the challenges by as they occur. Above all, don't assume your way is the only way or right way. There are many ways to be successful and Godly in your parenting.

How does he rate our parenting?

Weak   Neutral   Strong   Very Strong

How does she rate our parenting?

Weak   Neutral   Strong   Very Strong

Physically

Sex is a great gift of God that married people get to enjoy. God wants you to have a great sex life. However, sex has certain principles to be successful. Connect sexually on an intimate basis, talk during sex, don't be silent, and communicate about sexual matters outside of the bedroom. Be clear on frequency so nobody is confused or left hanging without clear information. Don't use sex as a weapon for power. Guys, women need emotional and spiritual intimacy to feel sexual toward you. They are aroused by how close they feel to you, not how handsome or in shape you are. So if you, as a guy, don't share your feelings and don't pray, then you are creating an environment where sexual desire can definitely decrease in your wife. So don't set her up for failure.

Ladies, sex is important for most men. When you make this a low priority, you are also setting up a relationship barrier that can have all kinds of negative impact in the marriage. If you can't resolve the issues, definitely get help so you can have the sex life God would like you both to have.

How does he rate our sexual connection?

Weak   Neutral   Strong   Very Strong

How does she rate our sexual connection?

Weak   Neutral   Strong   Very Strong

We covered several areas where principles, if applied, can create a very strong healthy marriage. Now I want you to see the areas of strength for focus.

	He				*She*			
Spiritually	W	N	S	VS	W	N	S	VS
Emotionally	W	N	S	VS	W	N	S	VS
Dating	W	N	S	VS	W	N	S	VS
Finances	W	N	S	VS	W	N	S	VS
Parenting	W	N	S	VS	W	N	S	VS
Physically	W	N	S	VS	W	N	S	VS

As a couple, I would like you to share insights together that this chapter has given to you. If you have strengths, celebrate these, and if there are areas to work on, be hopeful. There are always areas to grow in a marriage. This creation of marriage is ongoing for the rest of our lives.

I know there are days you may have questioned God's wisdom or your own in choosing this marriage, but as you work through the hours, days, or seasons, you come out more committed, bonded, and even love your spouse more.

Purpose of Marriage 8

I really like to know the "why" behind doing something. This desire increases in me especially if I am being asked to commit to something with my time or resources.

I remember when I was in Bible College that the "why" kept me going through late nights, interesting professors, and just above average food. I knew two reasons for why I was going to Bible College, and that kept me going year after year, while my old high school buddies were working and wasting their time.

Firstly, I clearly knew that God had told me to go to

Bible College. So I knew I was being obedient and that was really important to me as a new believer. Secondly, I knew this degree was going to help me as I helped others in future ministry. Understanding the purpose behind getting a degree helped me stay in the process until completion.

I think understanding the purpose of marriage can also help all of us stay in the process of marriage. I know there are days you may have questioned God's wisdom or your own in choosing this marriage, but as you work through the hours, days, or seasons, you come out more committed, bonded, and even love your spouse more.

Before we go down the path of the principles of marriage, I want to go down a path that has led people to pain and divorce because they truly did not understand the purpose of marriage from a Christian perspective. When you misunderstand the purpose of marriage, it can limit your ability to stay through the process because you're expecting a totally different experience or outcome.

So many Christians have bought a worldly idea of marriage hook, line and sinker. When this idea that "marriage is to make you happy" is purchased, it creates a truly wrong framework for that person in the marriage.

Let me digress a moment about being happy. Most reading this book live in the United States, or in the Western part of the world. As such, we are the richest people in the world. We are the most entertained, best fed, and have the most freedom to pursue our talents and dreams.

Most people who are turning these pages are Christians. As a Christian, the highest price in the world, Jesus Christ's blood, was paid so you could not only live this life to the fullest, but so you could also have eternal life. You also received His Holy Spirit in your life, which is absolutely amazing. Many of you attend a local church where you are preached the Word of God and have the fellowship of other imperfect believers.

If you can't be happy with all of these amazing blessings, don't put the burden of your happiness on your spouse. It is fully my job and responsibility to choose happiness if I want to be happy.

For example, it's 3.00 a.m. and I am writing these pages. I am very happy. I am outside with my dog, Moses, looking at the marvelous stars. I couldn't be happier. Someone else might choose to be unhappy, but I truly am happy penning these pages for you quietly before God.

My spouse can't make me happy or unhappy. It's not

> *When I truly understand God's purpose for marriage, I can sustain myself through any series of feelings and even be happier and more insightful into what God is doing with me through His purpose in marriage.*

job to choose how I feel or perceive a situation or my marriage. If, at my core, I thought the purpose of marriage was to make me happy, then when I am not happy, I could blame my wife or my marriage and be tempted to look for another person to see if that one would make me happy.

When I truly understand God's purpose for marriage, I can sustain myself through any series of feelings and even be happier and more insightful into what God is doing with me through His purpose in marriage. The secret of the purpose of marriage is in its very creation. Remember marriage is not a legal entity, rather marriage is an organic creation of three beings; a trinity on earth as it is in heaven. Let me use an analogy that you can relate to, to further understand the purpose of your marriage. Let's go to the creation of a child. To create a child the seed of a man penetrated the seed of a woman. When this man's seed dies totally to itself and God breathes His gift of life, it becomes a totally new creation, a child.

This child will have its own very unique DNA. Your marriage, as a creation by God, also has its unique DNA. This child has a destiny, as does your marriage. As each independent cell gives up its life totally, they merge into this new cell and there is a totally new creation.

In this very same way, God takes an independent

man with all of his experiences, foibles, dreams, and talents and he is to totally die to himself to create this new creation called marriage. Then God breathes on this death of each person and you have a marriage. The true purpose of marriage is to put to death your flesh, and make you Christlike, so you both can become one Christlike flesh. When you think of it, this is so awesome.

God calls Lisa and me to die to ourselves, and then He breathes on this process over the decades, and creates a Christlike creation called marriage. The purpose of marriage is to kill your flesh and create a resurrection of Christ's nature. Some die harder than others, but making us more Christlike is the goal of the miracle of marriage.

If your flesh is being put to death within your marriage, you are achieving God's purpose. Now this changes everything. If I am dying to myself, then I am being more successful in my marriage. If that's the purpose and the measure of my success, that changes everything. I'm not looking to be made happy, I am looking to serve and to die and my dying is up to me, not my spouse.

You might wonder why God would create a system where to have a new creation the old must be sacrificed. I didn't fully understand this myself but sacrifice, even total sacrifice, is a theme throughout the entire scripture, including Christ's total sacrifice for us to become new creations.

Christ, himself, didn't die somewhat to save humanity and create a new species of people called Christians. He died totally to give us eternal life and receive His Holy Spirit. The animals that were commanded to be sacrificed were killed totally to be acceptable to God. Even the whole idea of inheritance is predicated on the idea of death.

In the Old Testament, God gave the children of Israel the inheritance of the land. Often they were to kill everyone in the land to obtain their inheritance. In the New Testament we are given the nature of God Himself through Christ as our inheritance. To be Christlike we must die to our flesh, so He can resurrect His life through us. In my experience, His life is so much better than even the best of our human flesh.

So the purpose of being married is to die, that's exciting. Let me offer you two ways I evaluate if I am dying well in my marriage, and neither of these two ways require me asking my wife. Rather, I compare my heart and behavior to two places in scripture.

Both of these scriptures will be amazingly familiar, but when used as a grid for dying in the context of our marriage, they can shed new light on their application. The first of these scriptures is Galatians

5:16. This scripture gives to me a clear picture of what the fruit of God's Spirit is to be through me. As I read these qualities I can simply evaluate what is God's Spirit in my marriage toward my spouse, and what is still me.

Let's read this passage together and then walk through this, a little at a time. Let's start with a

> *"But the fruit of the Spirit is love, joy, peace, patience, kindness, goodness, faithfulness, gentleness and self-control."*
> *Galatians 5:16*

context. Paul is telling the Galatians how to live life. He exhorts them to live by the Spirit and not their flesh. He lists the characteristics of the flesh and now he outlines the characteristics or fruits of walking by the Spirit. "But the fruit of the Spirit is love, joy, peace, patience, kindness, goodness, faithfulness, gentleness and self-control."

Most of us love this scripture and have it memorized. However, let's walk through application of this scripture in the context of marriage. Firstly, fruit is for others. The apple tree doesn't eat its own fruit, people do. So the fruit of the Spirit is fruit we can offer our spouse. It's not for us or about us; it's about feeding our spouse a diet of spiritual fruit that grows through us to them on a regular, even daily basis.

The first fruit is love. I believe this is the core of all the fruit. If I love Lisa and I think more about her needs than mine then I am definitely more likely to give her the fruits of the Spirit to eat, instead of my fleshly fruits. So when I fail at having fruit, it's a failure of love at that moment.

All of us fail to love at times. Some of us have accidental fruits of the Spirit. We can, however, be intentional at loving and walking in the Spirit of love and offering its fruit. A spouse on a regular diet of love (barring addiction or a personality disorder) would grow on such a good diet from their spouse.

Joy comes in knowing God is up to something regardless of what the circumstances appear to be at the present time. Joy in a marriage is knowing at a core level that even in tough times, God is good, good can come out of this, and believing He is a rewarder of those who diligently seek Him. I know that sounds religious, but for me, I know God is able, so I trust Him. That lets me have joy in knowing somehow, someway He is working this all out and I might even have a good laugh one day about the incident or season. I get peace when I come from the place of trusting God in the circumstance. Patience is harder for me. I am a Type A, go, go, go guy. I have learned that patience can be sweet and it seems to help me give grace to Lisa and accept her more than trying to conform her to my wishes.

I have found patience comes when I make the incident more about serving Lisa. If I can lose myself in serving, I usually can reach patience. If I can challenge my belief that it's supposed to go my way, and be open to her direction too, I can also access patience. I am still learning and growing in this area of fruit. I do know this, when I get it right, Lisa sure appreciates it.

Kindness is loving and serving Lisa the way she needs it. Wives, this would mean serving in his love language as well. We all know how to be kind to our spouse, but being consistent can be challenging for all of us. Kindness may take some forethought or planning ahead. Most of us know what our spouse needs to feel loved. Kindness is consistently giving that gift. Kindness is also anticipating a need and meeting it before it is requested. I don't always get kindness right, but I can say that when Lisa asks for something to be done and I already did it, I feel kind. Goodness for me is staying in a right motivation toward my spouse.

To me, faithfulness has a whole lot more to do with being consistent. I need to do what I say, say what I'll do, follow through on commitments, pick up the kids when I say I will, and keep up with things around the house. Yes, faithfulness means romantic or sexual fidelity as well.

Gentleness is more of an attitude of service, rather than being superior. It also means not gloating when you happen to be right about something. Gentleness can make a marriage so much smoother day in and day out. There is no need to be harsh or rude toward the one who has committed their life to you.

Lastly, but not least, is self-control. For me this means I just don't have to say every silly thing I think. I can restrain my fleshly impulses that want to get even or make things fair. Self-control is a mature fruit. I definitely have to be able to discern the silly from important, and decide if something is or isn't worth a conflict. Self-control also means that it's not always about me. I think that's what makes self-control challenging to my flesh.

Marriage is a great photograph as to how I am doing with the fruits of the Spirit. This is the part of the relationship where my spouse gets the fruits of the Spirit, or the fruits of my flesh. I realized I am the chef and I get to decide daily which fruit my spouse receives. I have even had an accountability partner help me on this, and I was amazed at how much more I could choose to be more intentionally fruitful toward my wife.

Before I continue with the next scripture, I'll give you space to reflect on these fruits as they pertain to your spouse. You may or may not be more fruitful outside of the marriage, but I want you both to reflect on what kind of diet you are feeding your spouse. Give yourself a grade 1-10 or A B C D F in the fruits listed below.

Fruitfulness	His	Her
Love	____	____
Joy	____	____
Peace	____	____
Patience	____	____
Kindness	____	____
Goodness	____	____
Faithfulness	____	____
Gentleness	____	____
Self-Control	____	____

The other scripture that allows me to measure how

dead I am to myself within my marriage is I Corinthians 13:4-7. Although it has a couple of the same ideas as the afore mentioned Galatians reference, because it is also describing love which is God's nature, it also has a couple subtleties that help me see how dead I am, or am not, on any given day. Let's look at this together and then I will comment.

"Love is patient, love is kind. It does not envy, it does not boast, it is not proud. It is not rude, it is not self-seeking, it is not easily angered, it keeps no record of wrongs. Love does not delight in evil but rejoices with truth. It always protects, always trusts, always hopes, always perseveres. Love never fails."

I Corinthians 13:4-7

Love is patient, love is kind. It does not envy, it does not boast, it is not proud. It is not rude, it is not self-seeking, it is not easily angered, it keeps no record of wrongs. Love does not delight in evil but rejoices with truth. It always protects, always trusts, always hopes, always perseveres. Love never fails.

We have already covered patience and kindness, so let's get right into envy as it relates to marriage. It's so easy to be a victim in a marriage, and to feel like you got the bum deal because you're a man or a woman, and the other has it better. Love doesn't look at the positives of one role and the negatives of the other. Love accepts their role as God's will and training ground for them. Staying away from envying your spouse can keep you resentment free throughout your marriage.

Love does not boast. Here is the other side of envy. Love doesn't look at my strengths or roles in a one up manner, nor focuses on the negatives of the other. I guess if I could sum up these two points, love doesn't compare, period. I am not better than my spouse or worse than my spouse. Love sees the whole of marriage and knows both are equal, but have different contributions to a successful marriage and family.

Love is not rude. If you think of all the people you are rude to, to whom would you be the rudest? This is a question I have asked in marriage conferences. Most of us are surprised to realize the person who loves and serves us daily can often be the person we are most rude to. Rudeness is a choice to put me first and can be as simple as not letting the other person finish their sentence, or not being on time for my spouse. Love moves us away from rudeness into an other-centered approach to marriage.

Love is not self-seeking. If your marriage is all

about you, then you decide everything, you get mad when things don't go your way and you have difficulty serving others. You are hell to live with, plain and simple. Being selfish and self-centered makes trying to become a Christlike marriage very difficult. A person who stays self-seeking chooses to love themselves and to not love those around him or her. I realize we all are self-seeking here and there, that's human. Love is committed to serve and be aware of the other person. If someone hasn't made the basic decision that marriage is about serving their spouse, then their lack of love and immaturity can keep their marriage intentionally in pain. If this needs addressing in your life, as a husband or wife, please get accountability because this is not love of others, but of flesh that doesn't want to die.

Love is not easily angered. There is nothing like a spouse to give you the opportunity to be angry. They are resistant to change the way you want them to change, and they know how to push your flesh buttons to get a response. I am amazed at how little it takes to get a Spirit filled Christian angry at their spouse. Before I choose to get angry, I have found that asking myself two questions helped me get through this. Firstly, is this really a big deal? Secondly, will this matter in five years?

For me, anger is usually about it's not going my way. When I realize it's not supposed to always go my way and it's not all about me, it does help calm me down. Marriage gives opportunities to be angry; it's getting easily angry that love doesn't do.

There are times anger will be in a marriage. These conflicts, if handled well, can bring growth, closeness, and insight. Love can help us get through becoming easily angered so that we don't make little deals bigger than they need to be.

Love keeps no record of wrongs. Love doesn't need a laundry list to shame a spouse with. Love doesn't even keep a list. This is a really challenging characteristic of love. Women who remember better and with greater detail can struggle more with choosing to do history lessons. Love doesn't do history lessons. We are grateful that God doesn't do history lessons, but casts our sins as far as the east is from the west.

Here's a tip that helped me. Act like it's the first time your spouse has done a behavior that bothers you. Remember, marriage is to kill you. Remembering all these offenses is one thing; bringing them up to your spouse is another. Remembering that my role is to be my spouse's cheerleader really helps me here.

Love doesn't delight in evil, but rejoices with the truth. All spouses have a sin nature. Love doesn't focus on their weaknesses, but delights in their superiority in an area of life. Love rejoices in the truth. We are all sinners, all flawed and all loved. I rejoice that no matter what Lisa is, she is my friend and my wife.

Then there are the "always" of love in the scripture. These are great and challenging because sometimes you and I don't always want to do these for our spouses. Love always protects. Practically cover your spouse's weaknesses, even if their family members or friends get into some negative character evaluations of your spouse in humor. Always resist the temptation to join in.

Always trust your spouse. Believe they are competent, intelligent and capable human beings. When you come from this position it puts limits over instruction, reminding and parenting your spouse. Trust they will try to do their best and when, not if, they fail, give more opportunities to demonstrate future competence. If they are cheating on you or lying, then get help to address these issues.

Love always hopes. Love doesn't just see each day as a photograph of their spouse. Love sees a movie in which we are only in a scene. The movie of my spouse is awesome. What God is and will continue to do in and through my spouse over the decades is truly amazing.

Love always perseveres. This means you commit to the tomorrow. I know even on a rough day or night that Lisa and I will have a tomorrow. Usually the issues get clearer, smaller, and more manageable and we reconnect and verify our commitment and love to each other. You know what I am talking about. You have had many tomorrows because of your commitment to manifest love by persevering today.

It's here that the scripture mentions the last and

final "always" of love. Love never fails. The very nature of God is in our marriage. He is able to sustain us and mold us through this miracle we call marriage. When we both manifest His nature toward each other, we do not fail.

Let's do what we did in Galatians and grade ourselves on love as I Corinthians 13 describes love. Give yourself a grade to help evaluate yourself on how you are doing with these characteristics in your marriage.

Love	His	Her
Patient	____	____
Kind	____	____
Not Envious	____	____
Not Boastful	____	____
Not Prideful	____	____
Not Rude	____	____
Not Self Seeking	____	____

Not Easily Angered	____	____
No Record of Wrongs	____	____
No Delight in Evil	____	____
Rejoices with Truth	____	____
Protects	____	____
Trusts	____	____
Hopes	____	____
Perseveres	____	____

These two scriptures allow me to see if I am dying well. Since the purpose of marriage is death to myself, I want to know how I am doing. This also helps me not to focus on my spouse. I can commit to becoming more fruitful and loving in my marriage without my spouse's awareness.

I can decide to grow or not to grow in love. I can pray, get accountable, study the Word, practice new behaviors and attitudes, be a better person that

Christ can resurrect His awesome nature into, and fulfill the purpose of God in my marriage.

I really hope the discovery of the real purpose of marriage helps you. I have seen so many couples freed up after getting rid of the world's idea of "I'm supposed to be happy" and switch it to, "I'm supposed to be dead" which makes a world of difference.

The beautiful thing is that I have clearly not arrived. The more I focus on dying to myself and serving my wife and family, the happier I actually am. Amazingly, if we follow God's design, we get amazing results. So be encouraged, you are in the right marriage to fulfill the purpose of God in your life.

But have you ever really thought through the dynamics of God being your Father, and God being your spouse's God and creator?

Their Maker 9

In this part of our journey, I want to share with you a paradigm shifting idea that can help you look at your spouse with a totally new set of glasses. I have to start this journey with a story that you can relate to if your children are of marrying age.

Suppose you had two daughters. You loved them, cared for them, brought them up to be really godly young women. You sent them both to Christian college. Because they're godly and beautiful they attract young men. After dating a few times both of your daughters find their mate. You meet both men and they both profess to be Christians, love your daughter and follow the Word. A year later they both marry and the weddings were beautiful.

The first daughter's husband is exactly what he says he is. He is a godly man, he really loves your daughter, they pray together, they go to church, he is kind and patient to her. He brings your daughter back to you for regular visiting time together. Now I want you to ask yourself a question. How do you feel toward this young man who married your daughter?

My guess would be that you like him very much because he cares for your daughter. Regardless of what he does for a living, if he loves and cares for her, then this is largely going to determine what you think and feel toward him.

The second daughter's story is quite different. Since the wedding day, she has not been permitted by her husband to see you. You hear that he's drinking, cheating on her, and on occasion has been physically abusive toward your godly, beautiful daughter. He doesn't go to church, nor pray with her like he did before they married. He has defrauded her and your family. Now take a moment and think about how you would feel toward this young man.

My guess would be that you both would not like this young man at all. He has betrayed and mistreated your daughter, and damaged your entire family. I'm telling you this story because it helps lay down a fundamental principle about favor. Let's go back to when your children were very small through high school.

Along their road of development there is a coach, trainer, teacher or specialist in a particular field who takes notice of your child's gift inside of them. The gift may be athletic, art, debate, computers, or the love of animals. Regardless of the gift, this adult takes a positive interest in your child in the development of their gift. The child responds and becomes even better in this area of giftedness, maybe even reaching a goal and gaining recognition.

Let me ask you, how you would feel toward this coach or adult in your child's life? Again, my guess would be that you would like them very much. They would have favor with you, even if they had obvious foibles.

Reversely, if you had a child who had an innate gift or ability, and a coach, teacher, or adult was extremely critical or demeaning of your child and their gift, and this advanced to the point where it discouraged your child not to develop that gift. How would you feel toward that person regardless of how wonderful they were in general? You probably wouldn't have positive feelings toward them at all. You may not like them, or at least one could say they fell out of favor with you.

Favor is a simple thing. When someone cares for a loved one, you favor them. When someone is unloving or disrespectful toward someone you care about in your life, then they would have less favor with you.

Let me continue to show you a new paradigm. As western believers we often fall prey to our strong ideas of independence and seeing the world through our own glasses. For me to declare to you that God is your Heavenly Father would be easy for you understand. God is there for me, listens to me, cares for me, and desires the best for me. I think you get the focus. In the West, we see God reflectively as our God.

It is true that God is your God and your Father. But have you ever really thought through the dynamics of God being your Father, and God being your spouse's God and creator? That's right, the same intentional creativity God put into making you physically and designing your personality, He put into making your spouse. The same celebration and wonderment He has over you, He also has over your spouse.

God is not just your Father; He is your All-Knowing, All Powerful Father-in-Law God. That's right! You not only have God as a Father in this triune marriage, you also have the privilege and honor of having God as your Father-in-Law.

Take a minute and really, really think about this. God, who hears your prayers, thoughts, and the things you say in the car about your spouse, is your Father-in-Law. The heavens break open, God appears to you as the Father-in-Law God He is, and asks you how you're treating your spouse. He asks you why you're treating His child this way. What would your answer really be? Would you be happy to see Him because you treat His child, your spouse, really well? Would you be looking for the nearest thing to hide behind, because you thought it was acceptable to be consistently selfish, unkind, and unloving?

I live in this reality since God revealed to me that I was not only His son, but I was His son-in-law, and Lisa (my wife) is a favored daughter of His. Yes, that was a real wow moment to me. I remember thinking, "Wow, she is the favored one." Then it really hit me that the principle of favor we just talked about connected to God being my Father-in-Law. Because I am in a triune marriage then part of how God feels about me has to do with how I treat, care for, and love his daughter, my wife. That changed my life and my marriage.

This paradigm made it very clear that regardless of Lisa's behavior or attitudes (which hers are really pretty good, I might add), how I treat her determines God's favor in my life. I really believe this, so dishes, laundry, homework, cleaning up around the house are not a burden. Each of these gives me a practical way to show love to her. Sharing my feelings, praying, dating are all easy disciplines to have because I know my Father-in-Law God is pleased when I serve and share my heart and connect with her and bring her back to Him on a daily basis.

In my marriage, I aim to please the Father-in-Law God. I totally believe a good part of the favor of God that is on my life is because of the way I love my wife. I have had so many miracle opportunities in my life that anyone close by me knows God really likes me. I'm not special, but I do know beyond a shadow of a doubt I will one day stand before my Savior and my King and will have to give an account for how I treated His daughter.

When that day comes I want to hear, "Well done." Honestly my heart yearns for that day. I know God is a Father, so our relationships are most likely to be evaluated before my job or ministry. I want to know in my heart today that I please the Father-in-Law God. This makes a good part of my marriage between God and me, and not my wife and me.

I am, by no means, perfect. I feel the Spirit prick me when I goof up by being rude, retaliating, being impatient, or manifesting any other fleshly attitudes or behaviors. I also, at times, feel the smile when I get it right and am, for whatever reason, able to manifest love from my heart in a Christlike manner towards my spouse. Sometimes I smile back like a child who hit a homerun, and the child and dad smile together.

I want you to have the absolute best miracle of marriage that you can; knowing that (Hebrews 12:1) we are surrounded by a cloud of witnesses, helps me. I know I will be accountable for the treatment of my spouse, God's child. This helps me live a little wiser on a daily basis toward her, a child of God.

I hope that realizing God is your Father-in-Law helps you both to walk wiser and more loving toward God's child, your spouse. When you realize that you are married, not to a child of a president, but of God, it can help you be the best you can be for them!

Let me take you to a few application points to help you get this Father-in-Law concept deeply rooted into your Spirit. These are two very practical ideas you can apply to benefit from this paradigm shift.

This first principle really helps me personally and has helped countless couples who have applied it after attending our marriage conferences. This Father-in-Law God is omnipresent and all knowing. He was with your spouse all day, just like He was with you all day.

While you're driving home, or prior to when you know your spouse is coming home, pray. Don't pray to God your Father, pray to the Father-in-Law God. Ask the Father-in-Law God to impart His love, wisdom, nature, and gifts into you, to better love and serve your spouse.

> "Father-in-Law God, I am about to enter the zone. I have no idea what has happened to my spouse's life today like You do. Please give me Your love and Your heart for my spouse. Give me Your wisdom to see her needs and the needs around me. Give me Your strength to serve her fully and to give of myself to her. I give Your Holy Spirit full reign of my life and heart. Give me ears to hear, so I can obey You in serving her."

This prayer can sound something like this: "Father-in-Law God, I am about to enter the zone. I have no idea what has happened to my spouse's life today like You do. Please give me Your love and Your heart for my spouse. Give me Your wisdom to see her needs and the needs around me. Give me Your strength to serve her fully and to give of myself to her. I give Your Holy Spirit full reign of my life and heart. Give me ears to hear, so I can obey You in serving her."

Just take a moment and think how God is going to feel about you when you pray like this for love and wisdom to serve your spouse. I think just doing this can get Him to smile on you. If you actually follow through, and love, and serve, you can bet this would make God smile.

You know the feeling when your child has a situation with a friend or someone from school. You coach them, pray together and they follow through and it works. You're so happy and proud of them. I think that is the way God feels when we actually follow through serving our spouse.

This isn't complicated either. Men, you know she needs help around the house and with the children, whether she works or not. If you jump right in with a good attitude and even ask what needs to be done and do it, there is more happiness in your home. Ladies, you know he has worked all day and has a need for positive attention. Stop being so busy for a few minutes, kiss him real good, let him know he's all that, and you're glad he is home. Give him a real hug and affection before you shout off any orders, needs or negatives about what he didn't do. Affirm him first, and the evening can go better.

I know we all can get preoccupied with our own little world, however, that's only if you have a Father God.

When you are praying to the Father-in-Law God you can open your world to include your spouse, their heart, and needs. Living in a triune marriage with God is awesome.

The second principle I want to share with you on a practical basis to integrate this Father-in-Law God concept into your life, is what I call a check-in. In our recovery groups for sex addiction, intimacy anorexia and for their spouses, they have a check-in. They check-in on their recovery workbook progress, praying and other exercises. A check-in with the Father-in Law God would be similar to this. On a regular basis, whether weekly, biweekly, or monthly, have a check-in, not with God the Father, but with God the Father-in-Law. That's right, make an appointment and ask the questions:

1. How am I doing as a son/daughter-in-law?
2. How am I doing at manifesting Your love?

3. How am I doing as far as serving?
4. How am I doing with connecting my heart to their heart?
5. How am I doing at bringing my spouse to you in prayer?
6. How am I doing as a lover to my spouse?

> "God, not you, made marriage. His Spirit inhabits even the smallest details of marriage."
> Malachi 2:15

God cares about everything in our marriage. I love reading the verse in Malachi 2:15 in the Message Bible it says, "God, not you, made marriage. His Spirit inhabits even the smallest details of marriage." It is totally appropriate to have this check-in with the Father-in-Law God.

Of course it's really important that you listen. From my experience, God would rather instruct us, than correct us. I find in these evaluations that you can receive a soft word of correction that can change your attitude and behavior toward your spouse.

The best thing of all is that your spouse doesn't have to be involved with this process. This is just you and God. You can check-in with your spouse, but I find most of us have difficulty doing this without being defensive.

You can pray before you enter your marriage each day to better love and serve. You can also check in and get an early evaluation so your final grade can be awesome. There is nothing like learning from the Father about how to love the child He created for you in this marriage. I think these principles can help all of us hear "well done, good and faithful servant" from our Father-in-Law God at the end of our journey called marriage.

During the process of becoming one flesh, there are these intervals of desired change.

How to Change your Spouse 10

Almost everyone reading these pages has had a moment, at least one, where you wish your spouse would just change. It could be a small behavior such as leaving clothes on the floor, or things around the sink, the lack of support with the house or children's activities. Being married to an imperfect sinner at times can really have its moments!

You're probably smiling, and so am I, as I myself scroll through a few of these moments in my mind. I realize these moments are a part of every marriage on planet earth. I think this may be a part of becoming one flesh, which takes a lifetime. During the process of becoming one flesh, there are these intervals of desired change.

Usually these moments are from our limited perspective and we want our spouse to change. Sometimes unknowingly, God is working patience, or even better, long suffering into us, and utilizing our spouse's foibles to grind against something in us like pride or selfishness.

Let's go on a journey many couples have taken in the process of becoming one flesh. You may recognize some of these locations along the way where you may have tried to change your spouse. You may pass a town you have visited, or more appropriately, felt like you have lived in for years. You may pass a ghost town that you no longer visit, or that you visited once, and didn't like at all. Regardless, come along for the ride, and we will eventually get to a city that really works in changing your spouse.

Past Place

The first little town I want us to visit is Past Place. You probably remember the famous scene from Charles Dickens "A Christmas Carol." The ghost of Christmas past is the first ghost to awaken the sleeping Scrooge. They go on the journey of key events in Scrooge's life and he immediately wakes up.

The Past Place is where you were trying to change your spouse. Your spouse is about to have the opportunity to make the same mistake for maybe the one hundredth time in your marriage. The planets have lined up perfectly for this event to happen, so your instincts are alerted like the red lights at the railroad tracks before a train is about to come.

So what do you do? Like superman or superwoman you put on your cape and tights and fly to your spouse as quickly as you can to Past Place. Here you can remind your spouse gently, or not so gently, about similar past events where things have escalated. You take to the route of several incidences that have one or two people in common. Definitely they were at the scene of this historic event, and most likely you were there, as well or you would be able to remind them of the impact that it had in your life.

In Past Place there are two people involved: the flawed spouse and the spouse in spandex and a cape trying to help. Usually we take our flawed spouse to Past Places where there is no kryptonite. Past Place is usually an area of our own strength, so we can be tempted to be one up, superior, self-righteous, the teacher or role model. Rarely do we take our spouse to our own personal Past Place and show them our weaknesses and flaws, so that we are forced to re-experience it a hundred times or more.

I know most of us do it for...them. We are

trying to help...them. I get the rationale alright. But often when we take our spouse there, we expect the past to reoccur again. It's rarely to say, "I'm taking you here to rejoice with how well you have done in this area of our marriage. I want to place a monument to your success in this Past Place." That would be a really positive trip for both of you. In reality though, it's a place where the guest who was flown in doesn't feel so good afterward and unlike our character friend in Scrooge, they don't get to wake up. This isn't a dream; this is their life with you.

Angerville

Too many of us know this place called Angerville when it comes to trying to change your spouse. It's a strange town indeed when you look at the photographs. It looks like half the people have a sun burn. At a second glance it's not a sun burn at all, it's just the blood on the spouse's face when they arrive at Angerville.

The town is also strange in that only one person shouts at a time. That's the way they communicate in Angerville. There's also the photo of broken things all over the town. There are holes in the walls, and broken dishes all around the town.

The drink they offer in this town isn't water, but a cocktail called, "I am right" along with snacks of entitlement and superiority. These condiments can give tremendous energy to the visitors who take advantage of these free offerings.

Unlike Past Place, you don't fly here, you are transported. It's kind of like so many scenes from Star Trek. Captain Kirk, Spock and Dr. McCoy are standing on their circles and they get instantly beamed in. Angerville is similar to Captain Kirk telling Scotty to beam them back up, because there is no intelligent life in Angerville.

The residents of Angerville are very emotional. Their speech and logic may be very fast and uninterrupted, but when seen on instant replay they tend to go "outside of the lines" in football terms. The people in Angerville characteristically have issues with boundaries and respecting others. They are frequently mad, so whatever they do is justified. It's like drunks talking about the not so bright things they did the night before, after all they were drunk.

There is a problem after you leave Angerville, and that is usually regret. If you're proud, you still don't talk about your regrets, after all you were just angry, so you feel justified. If you're humble you have to wound your flesh and humbly ask for forgiveness.

If you're humble, and responsible, you will ask for

forgiveness and make a plan to prevent taking that drink of "I am right" in Angerville. Most of us have vivid pictures; some of us still visit here or unfortunately still live here.

Manipulative Manor

Unlike the other places we have visited, this is not a city or town, but a southern plantation manor you might see in Georgia, like in the movie, "Gone with the Wind."

Manipulative Manor can be owned by either spouse at any time. Manipulative Manor's title transfers very quickly and often without notice or even awareness. Manipulative Manor has some unwritten rules that have often been passed down from generation to generation. The first rule is the owner makes the rules; and the rules mostly apply to the subjects, not necessarily to owner of the Manor.

Also, the subjects (that's anyone but the owner at the time) are an extension of the owner, and are to do and believe things according to the worldview and experience of the owner. The owner has privileges, one of which is to dehumanize the subjects so they are more compliant servants, rather than amazing and competent children of God. The owner does make many assumptions like, "my ways and thoughts are right," and "I am innately superior."

There are countless techniques at the owner's disposal to get you to do or see things from their perspective, but the core thought is that, as a subject, you are being manipulated. As the subject, you don't really agree, but somehow you convince yourself that the owner knows what's best, and you don't want something worse to happen to you, so you submit your will to the owner.

The rules and answers can change on a whim, so both spouses may be guilty of believing they are the owner. This Manor is also a religious place where God is used to further the current owner's ideas, but God is not necessarily a real person with real authority in which the owner gives compliance to; that's for the subject.

You can see that Manipulative Manor is a place some of us go to in order to manipulate our spouse into change. After all, it's the best thing for them, is typically what the owner thinks. I know, as a counselor, when couples show me the DVD from their visits, it's pretty chaotic trying to get these systems and beliefs to really make sense. So if you get confused, you may be a subject in the Manor of Manipulation quite a bit.

Forcetown

This is another interesting town many couples have visited on the way to try to change their spouse. This town is like the New Jersey cop movies where the cops control everything that goes on. It's also like the old Westerns where the sheriff and what he says is the law, and if it's not obeyed there are some serious consequences.

Forcetown is about control. One person is in control, unlike Manipulation Manor where ownership changes. In this town, he or she is always the law.

In Forcetown, there's direct control of the spouse. He or she is to obey you just because and without question. The sheriff of Forcetown has several core beliefs. They are unquestionably superior due to bloodline, gender, money, gifts or any other reason they come up with. They hate the Scripture, there is no male or female in Christ Jesus (Galatians 3:28.) They grimace all the way through the chapter on the greater serves the weaker (Mark 10:35-45.)

Their core belief of being innately superior puts them in the position of their spouse not being able to challenge their position. When the sheriff is questioned, he or she wants to talk about the spouse's rebellion, or lack of submission, and not the flaws of their ideas or behaviors. Sheriffs rarely repent in Forcetown.

The sheriff changes their spouse through fear, intimidation, and a brutality that will eventually look questionable when Christ reviews this tape at the end of their life. There is a genuine disrespect and disregard for the spouse's personhood, heart, or life. Forcetown is a brutal place for anyone other than the sheriff.

If this is a place in your marriage, I pray you see the light of the love of Christ, lay down that self-righteous badge, and put the gun in the position of protecting your spouse, instead of intimidating them. No Christian should live here. Christ has called us to freedom and where the Spirit of the Lord is, there is freedom. In Forcetown, there is no freedom and little, if any, of the true Spirit of God.

City of Reward

This appears to be a prettier place than some of the other places we have traveled so far. The City of Reward is a golden city full of prizes from the easier life, if you follow the rules. The mayor of this town is a polished communicator and a great city planner.

If you do it his way, then he'll reward you with peace, or praise, a toy, or allow you a pleasure you like. City of Reward is calm as long as you are doing what is expected. The mayor doesn't command or dictate, but expects you to know better, and do the right thing as the mayor determines. The great thing about the City of Reward is you actually are given the rewards you were told you would receive.

However, the City of Reward has a dark side as well. If you don't do what is expected, you enter the area of the city that is dark and cold on Consequence Boulevard. This boulevard stands in stark contrast to the rest of the city where it is well lit and full of positive noise, good food and fragrance.

On Consequence Boulevard the buildings that exist are empty. You walk by the building of praise and there is no praise. You want to be touched or hugged, but nobody is there. Even the church is closed; your spouse won't pray with you, and intimacy is unavailable on this boulevard, as well as several of the other rewards your spouse knows you enjoy.

Consequence Boulevard is not eternally long. At any point you can walk a block back, follow Exception Alley, and you're back in the pleasurable City of Reward. If you are a spouse in this city, you have learned all too well about conditional love and passive punishment. You don't need to be perfect, but it sure helps if you live in the City of Reward.

The longer you live here, you figure out the almost unchangeable code based upon the "if, then" logic of the mayor. "If, then" logic is simple. If you do what is expected, then you are rewarded. If you don't, you are given a consequence. As a resident, and not the mayor, the quicker and more intelligent you are about the expectations (not rules mind you) the better your life will be.

Unfortunately, the only way out of this city is if the mayor has a heart expansion and accepts the flawed residents, and accepts that the residents have values and differences that can be equal, but different than theirs.

Shameville

This, sadly to say, is a place too many Christians have made a visit. Shameville is probably the darkest city we have visited so far. In Shameville you are brought here by yourself, by your experience, or by your spouse.

Let's talk about the founder of Shameville. Shame is not related to guilt. Guilt is "I have clearly done something wrong and I feel bad about what I have done." Shame is quite different. It is not, "I have done something wrong," but instead is, "I am something wrong, bad, ugly, unworthy, incompetent, a failure, no good or a loser."

Shame is attached to who I am, not an act of

doing. In Shameville, either of you can drive yourself or your spouse there. If you have a shame core, it can come out at anytime because it is what you believe about yourself. Your spouse might be making a valid observation, but you go to Shameville.

In Shameville you are bad, guilty and you cut off your resources to really hear and learn. You are judge and jury of what your spouse is saying and it's all bad, you are all bad and this is paralyzing you. Usually this core develops in childhood or adolescence. Often sexual abuse, rape, other abuse, neglect, or painful events occurred and you internalized these as bad things happen to bad people. Something bad has happened to me, therefore I am bad.

Shameville can also be accessed and capitalized on by a spouse. In this scenario the spouse is aware of your shame and capitalizes on it to change your behavior or beliefs. This may be a regular visit to keep the shameful spouse subjected throughout the marriage. This trip to Shameville can also be infrequent, brief, but used as a trump card by a spouse to get their way.

Regardless of who is driving, Shameville is not a good place to visit. I would recommend that the spouse with shame take a pit stop in a Christian counselor's office to be honest about the events connected to the shame, and process and heal these areas so you can't be taken to Shameville by yourself or your spouse.

Humble Valley

Wow, what a trip we've been on to try to change a spouse. I have mentioned a few of the major stops and some couples have stopped in other locations too, and have the souvenirs and bumper stickers to prove having been there.

Here's a place I found a little later in my marriage. It is a place that is guaranteed to create the atmosphere of change. I will warn you that to enter Humble Valley, you need to be able to unpack a few things to be able to arrive.

The first thing you will have to unpack is your belief that you can change your spouse. I realize you had an inkling that this thought was not true early on in your marriage. However we try to grieve this loss, we often stay in denial. I believe we can fully grieve over the power to change our spouse.

Not only do you have to leave the idea that you can change your spouse at the gate of Humble Valley, you're going to have to unpack any idea that it is your job to change your spouse. God has nowhere called us to do anything but love and serve our spouse. This is really hard especially if you are called and able to help others in some way with change.

The job of changing our spouse is one hundred percent the Holy Spirit's. His job is to come into a believer's heart and bring us to a place of conviction and desire to replace our flesh for Christ's nature. If the Holy Spirit chooses to use you, it will be in the nature of Christ, not control, manipulation, or one of the other places we have visited.

In recovery from addictions, an addict has to come to a place where he or she is powerless over that particular behavior. They can't do it by themselves, no matter how hard they try. They need the help of God and others. Even as Christians, we are powerless to change someone. Only they can choose to utilize the principles and support to change their life.

You have zero power to change them at all. That is really a day of freedom when you emancipate yourself from any belief that you or anything you do can create permanent change in your spouse. You not only don't have the power to change your spouse, you don't have the mandate or calling to change your spouse. I am called to love and serve my wife, Lisa. I have no calling to change her.

An added idea you may want to unpack is the idea that it's them that is being called to change. As westerners, we are more committed oftentimes to our idea of comfort, than the idea of character development. Unfortunately God has a reverse set of values. You know the ideas of being happy when you are being persecuted for My name sake (Matthew 5), and, when tried, rejoice because you're learning patience and perseverance (James 1).

God is committed to our character development, not our comfort. You can really rejoice since He has chosen the perfect spouse to give you the gifts of patience, perseverance, and the other gifts and fruits of His nature. I know it may feel unique to you, but isn't it interesting that your spouse has a flaw in the area that just grinds you. Do you think that's just by chance, or just the willfulness of your spouse? Or could it be a grand design to make you amazingly Christlike? You decide, but in Humble Valley you must be able to at least consider that it's you God is trying to change.

Well with some of these bags unpacked, I want to share with you a technique that has real potential to create changes. This technique is not for the faint hearted, that's for sure. It's a technique I have used with nothing short of miraculous results, and have had testimonies from people over my career stating how powerful this technique has been for them, and is in their life and marriage.

To start this technique you do have to fully purchase one key idea. That idea is that the God who created your spouse and you knows how to change you both. He knows you both more intimately and honestly than you know yourselves. He knows both of your strengths; He placed them there. He knows both of your weaknesses and blind spots. He also knows how to communicate through life, circumstances or people to get either of your attention. He, the Holy Spirit, is also called to create us in the likeness of Christ and convict us of sin. If you fully buy this idea, that He can change both of you, then Humble Valley is a place you can visit as often as you like.

Step One: Praise God

Step Two: Present a Clear Case

Step Three: Turn it Over to God

Here's the technique. Find a very quiet and secluded place to pray. This is a place you won't "accidently" be heard by your spouse. This is a time just between you and God. Remember, He is both roles, your Father and your Father-in-Law in this place of prayer. He is the fully engaged third person in your marriage.

Step One: Praise God

I find it's always good to start off with some praise of Him and genuinely be sincerely thankful for the gift in many ways your spouse is to you.

Step Two: Present a Clear Case

Then the next step is to lay out the issue or conflict as unbiased as you can. It's appropriate to share your feelings, pain, ideas and even bring up what your spouse may be feeling and thinking to God as well.

Step Three: Turn it Over to God

Then step three, and this is the difficult step, turn it over to God. Let Him know if you are the problem, you want to be corrected, disciplined, or given a word or idea to be part of the solution. However, if it is not you and you trust Him alone to change your spouse's heart on this issue, or to deal with that ongoing behavior or attitude, then one hundred percent be willing to take correction and repent, or be willing to let God do what God can do. Be and stay powerless to change them and be committed to love them regardless of the flaw. To be clear here, I am talking about normal conflicts and issues. I am not talking about abuse or ongoing infidelity. Those are issues for pastors, counselors, or the police.

I have used this technique many times. I must say I receive more corrections than Lisa changes. However, I am married to a really good hearted woman who rarely aggressively sins. My sin nature is more aggressive and needing of correction. I come out of that Humble Valley changed and more loving to Lisa. On the occasion where Lisa and I are at an impasse on a decision, I have seen God change her heart, or mind, or both and these are miraculous moments when my faith is in the third person in our trinity. Either way, I am improved as a spouse.

I hope you enjoyed our cross country trip on changing a spouse. I know most of you have found a familiar place along the way. My hope is we all can live in Humble Valley, committed to love our spouse through life, and enjoy the changes in ourselves and our spouse, as we marinate with the Living God over the decades within the miracle of marriage.

Over the span of your life, nobody other than Christ is more important than your spouse.

Three Roles of Marriage — 11

In this chapter I want to share a concept that has helped other couples become able to prioritize their marriage. I know, as well as anyone, life has a variety of demands. The demands of our time are spread out between family, friends, church, work, hobbies, self-care, money management, and some still have time for the news, along with additional hours of television each day.

I realize that for many couples the demands of life challenge their time management skills. I also realize that you have to make daily judgment calls about your valuable time. I've learned that I personally need to make clear boundaries to make the most important things happen. You have all heard the saying that the urgent can kill the important.

I want to help you make your marriage important. Firstly, after Jesus, your marriage is the greatest gift He has given you. Having a partner to share your life with is absolutely amazing to see and experience together. Secondly, out of this marriage comes the miracle of children and family. When the children leave to fulfill God's dream in their own lives, then it's just the three of you again – God, your spouse and you.

Over the span of your life, nobody other than Christ is more important than your spouse. Here I want to convey to you what I call the three roles of a marriage.

Role #1 Friends and Lovers

The role of friends and lovers is the foundational role of any marriage. Let's look back to the season of dating your spouse; the two of you became friends and you had someone to talk with. You encouraged each other in the struggles you were going through. You could see each other's strengths clearer than you could see the weaknesses. Do you remember really liking to be with each other? I remember feeling honored that Lisa would be with me and give her time to me. Our time together was the highlight of our week.

Then you started to kiss, and WOW, the lover part of the friendship was over the top. Just to hold her hand, or stroke her hair, or to be kissed by her made my life just so good to be alive. This friendship/lover role is often lost in many marriages because couples fall out of the discipline of sharing quality time together, sharing each other's feelings, praying together and dreaming. I have had so many couples in counseling and at conferences tell me that they fell out of love. I look at them both and say, "You didn't fall out of love, you fell out of discipline."

They look shocked and I simply ask, "Can you do a few things regularly for sixty days and see if I am right or wrong?" If they say yes, I give them the principles we talked about earlier, praying together, sharing feelings, praising each other, dating, and regular sexual connection with their eyes open, lights on and having nurturing conversation. I have never, in twenty years, had a couple who actually did the work, call or email me stating that they were still not in love.

When you keep the foundation of your relationship strong, then the rest is much easier. This friendship/lover relationship is the life giving oil that keeps marriages buoyant and more fun. If however, this friendship/lover relationship becomes neglected, then every role built on this foundation is impacted. The both of you can get unhappy, and still function moderately, but it's not what you would call fun.

What I have found happening with couples is that when they keep the foundation of their marriage a priority, then they both feel more loved and respected. In a marriage, these two ingredients, go a long way in raising a family and solving life's challenges, both in the present and future.

Remember these feelings are a result of actively focusing on the foundation of your marriage. Ask yourself and each other how you perceive the foundation of your marriage. Would you say very strong, strong, neutral, weak or very weak?

Before you go through the rest of the chapter, close

the pages of this book and have a real heart to heart about this foundation in your marriage. If you need to apply new disciplines to get new results, that's a great start. If you just need to enjoy where you are, that is great as well.

Role #2 Husband and Wife

The second role gets a little more complicated. Remember as God was creating, He kept getting more and more complicated along the way. So, as amazing as we humans are, marriage is still a step beyond, since it is His last creation. In this role of husband and wife, management and values collide with resources, time restraints, and two evolving personalities with quite a different universe of experiences.

The second role from a counselor's perspective is really quite interesting. Most couples never actually sit down and say this is how we are going to do x, y or z.

Usually what happens is largely unintentional and quite honestly, happens by default rather than actual consideration.

Each couple evolves creating systems to manage time, money, relationships, sex, entertainment, and it is usually a nonverbal decision making process. Remember, most of us come at this task with two daunting handicaps. First, most of us are young when we get married and second, we have zero experience navigating such a complex interdependent relationship that demands serving and unselfishness at such an advanced level. Let's walk through these major clarifications that need to be worked through in the second role of marriage.

At this time I'll ask which one of you makes the decisions. Then, why does this person get to decide? How long do they get to decide? Do they decide because of gender? Do they decide because of giftedness? Do you both have to agree on everything? Can one person take the lead on something without the other getting offended? How is God consulted in a decision? Do you use your resources to solve a problem or to attack the other person? That's a lot of questions, you may be thinking. Yes, and I could go on for a couple more pages and I am only on one aspect of the husband and wife role. That aspect is how are decisions made and why?

I chose this one first because as a counselor I know two things. Most couples never even know how they make decisions. Secondly, I have a hard job, unless I know how this system works. Does he make all the decisions, does she, is it shared or topical, are they accountable to anyone on their decisions?

I think before a veterinarian does surgery on an animal, he or she ought to know if it's a cat or a dog first. So an important aspect for a couple in the second role of husband and wife is to clarify who or what process is followed in making decisions regarding the multiple issues pertaining to marriage.

Again, this might be a really good place to put your finger in the book and talk through this. You most likely have been married for a while and whether you have ever spoken it out loud, a decision process has evolved. So it's time to give this process a name and an evaluation as to whether it is the best process for your marriage.

Time is a commodity and none of us know how much we have. It's also a commodity that we want to utilize under the direction of the Holy Spirit. As young couples there are time demands from the job, the school if you're in college, both of your families, both of your friends and mutual friends, and time for each other, and then time for yourself. Oh yeah, and then time for God as well!

How a couple navigates the management of time is critical to the long term health of the marriage. Is time a mutual decision or an individual decision? Is time bullied for, manipulated for, or is it respectfully allotted? Is time always allotted due to circumstances, or crisis, or is it actually thought out like a regular time for prayer, dating, sex, and alone time? Do we live a day at a time, week at a time, month or year at a time? Is vacation time valued or not? How much time do we give to church, community, friends, hobbies or just being alone? Is time with friends, alone or together, a value or a threat to your marriage?

Again, often these questions are not answered ahead of time. The time management system just evolves. We don't know why we do our life in the chaotic or orderly way we do, we just do it.

One of the most interesting exercises I have noticed on evaluating your time management was to evaluate your values. On a blank sheet of paper, write your top five or ten values, ranking the top one as the most important and go down to your lowest. Then flip the paper over and categorize your time the way you actually use your time, the top being what you spend the most time on and the last being what you spend the least.

It's a great exercise for the client or couple to see if their core values are expressed in actual time or if their time and values are incongruent. This would be another time to stick your finger in the book and just talk. If you need to make some adjustments in your time management to strengthen your marriage, then make the corrections to improve your miracle of marriage.

Money is also a crucial element in which systems of beliefs and management just evolve early in marriage. Like so many of these systems, they evolve in a reactionary or circumstantial manner as opposed to a great master plan of thought. After all, rent is usually due within a few weeks of the marriage.

Do we tithe? Do we save early on? Do we invest? When do we buy a large ticket item? How much debt should we have? What do we believe about paying off credit cards? Do we have a budget? Are we accountable to anyone? Does one person do it all? If we write checks, does that person make all the decisions? How do we, or do we, monitor our spending? What about house, food, college funds, retirement, and leaving a legacy?

When you're just trying to pay the rent, you don't think through the long term ideas of money or its management. However, the systems you create can last a life time. Are we emotional or logical about money? These early decisions can lay a framework of good or bad principles when it comes to this second role in your marriage.

Like the other subjects we covered, this might be a good time to close the book and chat about money and your marriage. As you're building the beams of your miracle, you want to make sure you think through your choices and create the best possible decisions. If you need help, get some books in this area, take a financial class at your church, or see a financial counselor. This is a very important aspect of management for any marriage.

Sex is a great gift in the miracle of marriage. I know from listening to couples that this system is one that often stays in the dark. Even though a couple has had sex many times, they often have never ever talked about sex and what they really want in their marriage.

How much sex should we have in a week? What can we do or not do? Who initiates, both or just one person? Why? Do we have sex in the dark or with the lights on? Do we talk during sex? Is God present? Are my expectations legitimate? Is the husband or wife using pornography? Do we make this a priority? Do we schedule sexual encounters to have some time? Do we use foreplay, what kind and for whom? Am I being honest about sex with my spouse?

Talk about a conversation worth having! I have seen many couples truly damaged because of the years of silence about sex. This is a subject that must be thoroughly discussed. I recommend you do this in a public place, not at home, definitely not the bedroom, and not before or after sex. If you need help here, you can make a counseling appointment.

Sex is powerful in your marriage. This part of the

miracle of marriage is sacred. However, several aspects of the roles of the husband and wife have systems that evolve without great thought. This time I would not say close the book and chat. I would say set a time this week or next to meet in a public place with some privacy to really open the discussion of how you want to manage sex in your miracle of marriage. If this is already a strength in your relationship and you have worked this out, just enjoy your accomplishment in this area of your marriage.

Entertainment we have discussed already in this book. Needless to say, the system and values regarding entertainment started early and when you both were young. Entertainment in general has grown more ungodly over each decade. These boundaries, as far as how much a week and what types are acceptable, really need to be evaluated in a clear manner. Stopping here and being clear would be a benefit for you both just to be sure you're in agreement on both the quantity and quality of entertainment.

Relationships will be the last area that we will discuss as it relates to the husband and wife roles of your marriage. This subject, like others, has various aspects that need to be examined to be sure you're in agreement.

Do we invest in same sex friends? If so, how much time? What are boundaries on these friends, and their beliefs, and life practices? What are the boundaries for professional or opposite sex relationships? How much time do we have for relationships with other couples? Do we have mentors? Do we have people we are accountable to? How much time do we have for church relationships? Are we involved in community activities, volunteering, and political groups?

The area of relationships will definitely bring both of your values in to play. This area will change and evolve as you go through the various stages of life, pre-children, children, post-children, and retirement. How you have decided to manage your present relationship issues may have never even been spoken about. It is important that you are clear on where you are today and agree on these relationship factors in your life. Sharing in relationships with others is great, but only in balance, like everything else in life. So like the other subjects we've discussed, take some time to chat about this one as well.

Role #3 Parenting

This is the third role of the marriage. As God created marriage to be a miracle that happens over decades, I am sure there was great wisdom in saving parenting for the last role of the marriage. I'm not sure, but I think the friend/lover role prepares you to become willing to make this unselfish commitment to die to yourself and become a new creation.

The second role is when that commitment, to die to yourself, is really challenged. I don't think anyone realizes how selfish they really are until they get married and start working through all the aspects of marriage. Pregnancy alone can really stretch a couple with multiple opportunities to die to self and grow to be more like Christ. You only thought you were all together and Godly, then all of a sudden comes a lesson on steroids about dying to self. Sleeplessness, more responsibility, and more questions face the couple as they behold this helpless angel that is challenging what remains of their flesh.

So who gets up at night? Why? Who changes diapers, helps with homework, and does the laundry? What are our roles? Whose ideas are the best and why? How do we make decisions, emotionally, with information, or with help from others? Do we admit when we make mistakes? Do we blame the spouse for imperfections? What about diet, exercise, bed times? The list goes on and on, college, cars, girl or boyfriends, their friends, what church is best for them?

These dialogues you will have for decades. Then as an extension of this role you get to be in-laws and grandparents. How involved are you going to be and why? Do you honor this couple when you disagree with their decisions? You can clearly see this is an important role that most marriages will go through. Here I recommend you read everything you can get your hands on. Talk to parents that are a stage or two ahead of you, and you like their children. Consider your gene pool issues. Question how you both were raised, keep what is good, and decide what's best, not who is right. Remember, conflicts over parenting are opportunities to become one flesh.

As a couple, keep you roles in order. Stay friends and lovers, this is the foundation of the miracle of marriage. Your marriage has three people, so stay friends and lovers with God. As you are able, work out as many issues as clearly as possible. Involve God and others for the spots that are challenging your humility. To ask for help will quicken the one flesh process.

In parenting, do your best, expect mistakes, and realize God is bigger than you both. He is committed to that child as well. As you bring them up in the triune relationship they will also know God and depend on Him as they journey through life.

I hope this short walk through these roles has sparked some insight and discussion. I pray these discussions lead to decisions, and the decisions lead to disciplines, and disciplines lead to a greater, stronger, more of a life giving miracle of marriage for both of you.

We can marinate in the

Word and Presence of God.

Pitch of Praise 12

I want to release to you a lifetime tool that, when used consistently can change and invigorate your marriage. Before I do that, however, I need to build a framework of understanding as to possibly why or why not you both are not actively, or should I say, intentionally utilizing this tool in your miracle of marriage.

I want you to take a journey back, and for some of you, way back. I want you to go back into your growing up years with mom and dad if you had both parents. I want you to consider the word atmosphere when you were five, ten, fifteen years old. Think back as to what words your soul was marinated in as a developing person.

You know what I mean by marinating I hope. Today is July 4th, when I am writing this chapter and my family is still asleep. Today is a day when men and women think at least a day ahead in preparing their steak, chicken, kabobs, seafood or whatever else they may enjoy on the grill.

For many of my Fourth of July chefs, this included thinking through and preparing the meat or seafood. They may have created a sauce, or bought it at the local store. They mixed it up, and then took that meat, and placed it in the environment of that sauce. Now the meat was neutral before the marinating. However, after a day or so that meat absorbs the flavor of that sauce. The sauce may be a sweet barbeque, a lemon or lime sauce, pepper or hot sauce. Whatever the sauce is, the meat will have that flavor.

I think you understand the marinating analogy. You and your spouse's souls were marinated in words regularly, daily by your parents. Depending on the primary ingredient of the sauce, you may have come into the marriage marinated in a certain flavor. I want to talk about three large categories of sauces I have seen people marinated in as young souls. As a child or adolescent you didn't get to pick the sauce you were marinated in. The choice of the sauce was one hundred percent your parents. They may have been just repeating the old family recipe that they learned from their parents.

As believers we get the option to marinate ourselves in another sauce. We can marinate in the Word and Presence of God. That's really good sauce, and can be the ingredient that can transform our lives and marriage. Now let's look at the three sauces you may have been previously marinated in as a little person.

Sauce #1 Criticism

Unfortunately this is a sauce too many of us growing up were marinated in. Our parents may have come from the same sauce and this sauce may be a family sauce going back hundreds of years. In this sauce you are told "you're stupid, not good enough, fat, lazy, can't do anything right, ugly, not good at..."

If you didn't grow up in this family, that's good. However, if you did, some of this sauce may have seeped deep into the pores of your soul. You may actually come to believe these lying statements of your parents or care givers. You may even become resistant to praise. You may not even really believe that God or your spouse really loves you. If they knew your flaws, they would reject you in a heartbeat.

The symptoms some of my clients have had from this type of sauce can damage their miracle of marriage.

Firstly, they can develop a negative lens on people in general and specifically on their spouse. They tend to focus on the small percentage of their spouse that is less than perfect and see them through that primary lens of criticism. Some spouses think this is helpful, regardless, it can become a situation where you are marinating your spouse in the wrong sauce. Secondly, they can't allow genuine praise deep into their heart. They block the seeds of praise so they can't grow into their heart and generalize that they are an awesome child of God.

Imagine marinating in a sauce of, "you're not good enough." Overtime this can actually become a core belief. If this becomes a core belief, the spouse can bring a black hole into the marriage. They can't be filled by God or their spouse, because they may be on a mission to protect or fulfill that they are not good enough or worthy.

If criticism is the sauce you were marinated in, and possibly suffered abuses of various types, this is your work to do to have a better marriage. I remember it was a few years into my marriage when Lisa rolled over and said I love you and I finally really believed her. Believing she loves me and is on my team has changed our marriage dramatically. Remember the saying, "If life gives you lemons, make lemonade." The difference is just the ingredients.

Sauce #2 Silence

I believe some children are marinated in the cruelest voice of all, that voice is silence. In this family you are seen and not heard; you are not spoken into or over. You're in a family where you feel more managed than related to. You don't hear bad things, you just don't hear anything. Your heart was made to connect and receive feedback, but it's just not there.

Maybe you grew up alone and quite disconnected from one or both of your parents. You wonder why, but more often, you just conclude that it's just the way it is. You also may conclude that you just didn't need anything from them anyway. Even if you wanted praise, validation, or connection you're just going to be massively disappointed. Once you conclude you don't need or even want praise, you can make another huge poor conclusion that can damage your life and your marriage.

You can conclude year after year of not getting praise and still living, that others and especially your spouse doesn't need praise to live either. They shouldn't need it and you might even conclude they are weak and needy even for asking for this. This would be a normal soul's response if marinated in the sauce of silence. To pass this sauce along to our spouse is the saddest repercussion of this sauce. The victim of silence now becomes the perpetrator of silence condemning their spouse to the hopeless feelings of never getting connection from you.

Sauce #3 Praise

In a family where praise was the sauce, the child is regularly nurtured and celebrated. In this family they are told, "You are amazing, awesome, incredible, smart, competent, creative, persistent, you make good choices, and God has amazing plans for you." This child is fortified on a regular basis by being affirmed. This child has a strong foundation giving them a natural resistance going into life.

Although this experience for the child is actually awesome for them, this sauce can have a sneaky weakness. This child believes they are worthy of praise and really have a need for affirmation from their spouse. This spouse thinks they are worthy to be seen, heard, and praised regularly. They expect the environment of praise to continue in marriage. If their spouse, however, was marinated differently they could be sentenced to significant disappointment. They will ache for the words, "you are amazing, awesome" and the occasional dribble "good job." If they have to continually ask to be praised, a trivial word here and there will seem like a drop in the desert to them. Unfortunately we don't get to go back and do things differently. However, we do get to change today and cook our marriage in the sauce of our choice. You can see the value of knowing the sauce in which you were marinated. This can really be helpful as you walk through the next few ideas to enhance your miracle of marriage.

Your Decision

Most of us when we became parents made the decision to do things differently, in some cases way differently, regardless of the sauce we grew up in. I have heard countless parents tell me that they decided these children of theirs were going to be raised differently and they were going to be loved every day. They chose to praise and connect to their children, or spend quality time, buy them gifts, or countless other reversals from the parenting they received growing up.

As Christians we also get to choose to be marinated in the Presence, the Person and the Word of God. We can decide to marinate in His love for us and allow His voice, His truth, His nurturing of us into all the pores of our soul and be changed by His person in our life. This is a major decision as Christians that we can choose to be impacted by God who loves us, regardless of what sauce our parents gave to us.

A decision I have rarely seen in my office is what kind of primary voice or sauce you are going to be toward your spouse. We are cognizant of deciding to be better parents, but what about the sauce you are providing to your spouse?

Think about this for a moment. Your spouse was with their family from birth to 18 or so years. You marry them in their twenties and if you stay married for life, which can be fifty to seventy years. That means your sauce, whether it is criticism, silence or praise is the dominant sauce your spouse experiences throughout their life.

Remember, as a child they had no choice in the sauce. They also have no choice as to what sauce you provide. They are blessed or cursed on a regular basis by the sauce you provide to them. They can't choose the ingredients you feed them, whether you choose your flesh, the devil, or the Spirit of God; they simply have to experience your choice of sauce toward them.

Think for a moment how every word we speak toward our spouse will be evaluated. If that's the case, which scale would weigh the heaviest in your word assessment toward your spouse? Would you weight heaviest on criticism focusing on the negative, silence, not really connected or engaged leaving them feeling tolerated or managed, or would it be in praise of them on a regular basis?

Stop and really think what Jesus would say about your sauce toward your spouse. One day He will assess you on this issue, but what would He say today? Take a moment and really think this out. As Christians, we won't have the excuse of our parents because we could have chosen to give God authority over our hearts and lives.

As you consider this I want you to consider that God has given you the responsibility of being the primary voice in your spouse's life. This is as great a responsibility as that of being a parent, and that is to intentionally marinate your spouse for their betterment.

Let's take a moment and see if we can determine the Father's voice. Our Heavenly Father, the third person in our miracle of marriage, definitely has a primary voice toward us. I want to take you to two familiar stories in the Scriptures where we see a photo of God the Father with God the Son. Rarely do you capture two or three of the Godheads in one photo opportunity, but there are a couple we can look at and clearly see God's primary voice towards Jesus.

The first of these photo ops is at the baptism of Jesus. Before we go there, let's think about the heavenly context of this event. Way back, after the fall, the plan of the Father and the Son and the Holy Spirit was for man to be redeemed.

The Son was sent to destroy death and give eternal life to all who would believe. The Son was conformed to a womb, walked as a toddler, worked in Joseph's woodshop, sweated, and ate like all other humans, but was fully divine.

"As soon as Jesus was baptized, He went up out of the water. At that moment heaven was opened, and He saw the Spirit of God descending like a dove and lighting on Him. And a voice from Heaven said, 'This is my Son, whom I love; with Him I am well pleased.'"

Matthew 3:16-17

Then Jesus was about to walk into the fullness of His ministry on earth and this baptism was like a heavenly bar mitzvah. Let's read Matthew 3:16-17.

"As soon as Jesus was baptized, He went up out of the water. At that moment heaven was opened, and He saw the Spirit of God descending like a dove and lighting on Him. And a voice from Heaven said, 'This is my Son, whom I love; with Him I am well pleased.'" God the Father could not stay in Heaven. The Son was having a major life event and he just had to speak to Jesus, not in private, but in public. He let everyone hear Him say that Jesus was loved and that God was pleased with Jesus.

I am sure this was heartwarming to the Son, like the dad at a football game praising his son for a good play out loud and in front of everybody. This was God the Father saying, "That's my boy and I am very happy with Him."

"While He was still speaking, a bright cloud enveloped them, and a voice from the cloud said, "This is my Son, whom I love; with Him I am well pleased. Listen to Him."

Matthew 17:5

A second photo op is found in the transfiguration of Jesus. In Matthew 17, Jesus takes Peter, James, and John and literally transforms before their eyes into God the Son. In Matthew 17:5 it says, "While He was still speaking, a bright cloud enveloped them, and a voice from the cloud said, "This is my Son, whom I love; with Him I am well pleased. Listen to Him."

Again we see the public affirming of Jesus to the disciples that God the Father loved Jesus and He was pleased with Jesus. It is really clear to determine the primary voice of God as outrageously nurturing. He is a praiser. He is not a critical or silent parent at all. He is a lover of all His children, including your spouse. So as you are considering the sauce you want to marinate your spouse in, you may want to think about the Father's sauce.

A second consideration while you're deciding your sauce is to decide your role toward your spouse. I find if a person defines their role with their spouse, then that gives them clarity on their primary voice toward their spouse.

One role is the critic. Their primary role is to spot the flaws, short comings, mistakes and poor judgment. You may be a critic whose motives may be to help or improve your spouse, or be a critic just to be a critic, or to intentionally make your spouse feel less than you. If they are less than you, you get to be greater, make more decisions, and your flaws don't get noticed or discussed. Remember, roles are chosen, so you can choose and unchose any role you have previously assigned yourself.

A second role toward your spouse may be the role of a ghost. They can feel you there, but you're not really seen. You are not critical or nurturing, you're silent. You have decided the path of least resistance, non-involvement. You decide it's just better not to say anything. Your spouse is on their own emotionally, or spiritually, or both. You told them you loved them when you married them and you'll let them know if you change your mind. Your silence is a sentence of pain and cruelty. This role of a ghost is the most damaging of any role. You have condemned your spouse to a religious prison that they cannot leave, or stay, or know if they are truly valued as they sacrifice their life in service of you. Regardless of why you would choose this role, you can change, even if it is hard work to move toward an intentional and engaging role toward the child of God you married.

The third role is the cheerleader. The cheerleader is attentive to the positive. The cheerleader lets them and others know regularly of their positive attributes and success. The cheerleader role is, "I am here to see your strengths. I am here to reflect them back to you so you know two things: I am madly in love with you and you absolutely please me." These messages are verbally spoken almost daily and in so many little and large ways that your spouse, if their pores are open, they are being marinated in praise.

For me, I actively decided to be Lisa's and my children's cheerleader. I actively praise them daily and regularly so they know I love them, I am pleased with them, and that God has created each of them, including Lisa, with an amazing purpose.

I know they are not perfect, neither am I, and I am loved and celebrated by the One who is perfect. This is the role I have intentionally decided on.

My hope is you will take a moment and really make a decision, not a light decision, but a heart covenant decision to decide your role and your voice toward your spouse. They will be marinated by you, so decide the flavor of the sauce. If their pores are open, it can impact them significantly.

You may or may not be very good at giving and receiving praise. I highly recommend giving your spouse eye contact and letting them know how awesome they are. Also, make sure they say thank you, so you know they let the sauce of praise into their heart. Even a good sauce, if not tasted, can have little impact. Training your spouse to say thank you lets you both know they tasted the sauce that you intentionally made for them.

If you have never done this, direct praising, it's really awesome. Secondly, make a long list of why your spouse is awesome, what are their strengths, and how they are a blessing to you. Keep this in your Bible so you can thank the Father for them. This can be an intentional way to see your spouse through your Father's eyes and get His lens on your spouse so you can be His voice toward them, all the days of their life. How do you think God would feel toward you now that you are praising his daughter or son? He made them and He thinks they are amazing. Praising them before His throne, I am sure is a positive feeling for God. This lets Him know you are grateful for your spouse. So praise them to their face, in front of others, and before God, and you will be amazed how much more you love and value your awesome spouse. Happy marinating!

A couple that doesn't believe God is God already has limitations in their miracle of marriage.

10 Commandments for Marriage 13

Honestly, when you flip through the pages of the Bible, there are a few stories that incredibly capture the heart and story of God. We have the stories of Creation, the Fall, the Patriarchs, and then the Exodus story. The Exodus is one of my favorite stories in so many ways. I remember Charlton Heston playing Moses in the old movie The Ten Commandments and the great scene where God gives Moses the Ten Commandments. There Moses is with the core message God wants His people to live by. These Ten Commandments are the hub of much of western thought, law, and how to live life.

As someone who has worked with marriages for more than twenty years, I have heard endless sermons on marriage and on various parts of the Ten Commandments, yet I have never heard anyone take God's core thoughts on life and apply them to His final creation, marriage.

So I thought this would be a stimulating conversation to have and walk through these ideas and see what principles from the Ten Commandments we can apply to marriage. I hope both of you can hold hands, walk through the garden of the heartbeat of

> "I am the Lord your God, who brought you out of Egypt, out of the land of slavery."
>
> Exodus 20:2

God, and look as we discuss each commandment separately. I hope this walk in the garden stimulates conversation to highlight your marital strengths and maybe see ideas that can even strengthen your miracle of marriage.

Before we start on the commandments, we should look at what God says before He gives the commandments. He delivered His people from Egypt. He declares this statement before He starts the commandments. "I am the Lord your God, who brought you out of Egypt, out of the land of slavery."

In the beginning of this dialogue God establishes who He is, He is God and He is responsible for their deliverance. I love that He starts this whole dialogue with who He is, that He is God, Lord, and responsible for our deliverance. When we talk about the miracle of marriage, you must believe He is God. He is master of you totally, and He delivered you from singleness into your miracle of marriage.

He is God

A couple that doesn't believe God is God already has limitations in their miracle of marriage. A couple who doesn't firmly believe that the third person in their marriage is God Almighty will try to fill that perceived gap with something else. Often they can wrestle as to who gets to be God. They come up with random reasons why they should be God, be it gender, gifts, abilities, money, family or origin, or just because they are a better bully, manager, planner, or more responsible. The reasons why a Christian man or woman wants to be God are endless. However, the characteristics of a couple who has this vacuum are very easy to spot. The person who wants to be God will:

- Demand compliance and obedience
- Use anger, silence, and controlling behavior to punish
- Their ideas are to be heeded quickly
- They don't tend to apologize easily
- They are arrogant
- They don't tend to humbly seek help from others
- They are not usually quick to see their sin nature

He is Master of You

If He is God, He is Lord of me. He tells me what to do. I am not God. I am a servant; I take orders from the one who is God. When He is master, He is master of all. He is master of our hearts, attitudes, behaviors, beliefs and we are to be about His business in our marriage. When someone believes God is master, he or she is a servant to God in their marriage. When someone doesn't have God as master, he or she looks to be served. This is a real clear way to see if God is Lord in your heart and in your marriage. For most of us becoming a servant is a process. A servant embraces the process and calling to serve as it relates to a master. Someone who wants to be served resists all notions of this calling to be a servant.

"It is not good for the man to be alone."
Genesis 2:18

He is Deliverer

God, Himself, delivered me from, "It is not good for the man to be alone." He delivered me from my world of selfish slavery into the miracle of marriage. He created us both for each other to grow into His image. He gave us both strengths and challenges to walk a journey of intimacy with us both in our marriage.

Knowing that God did this miracle called marriage is at the core of my being. I know God put Lisa and me together. Even in a challenging moment, I know God created our marriage and He will deliver one of both of us from our flesh, stubbornness, or short sightedness. This core belief that God is in our marriage anchors me to hold on and see what He is doing in us or in my heart to bring us into His image.

#1 You shall have no other gods before me.

I love this. God first declares I am God, Lord, and deliverer and His first command is to have no other gods. I love the logic of God. If He is God, there is no other. To have other gods of any kind would be to live in a fantasy or delusion of some type. God doesn't live in fantasy, but in reality, and a reality that He alone is God.

We can theologize this command or we can ask ourselves some questions. When in trouble do I go to God? Do I behave as if I believe He is God? Do I seek and worship Him regularly acknowledging that He is God? If someone was doing a DVD of my life, would there be enough evidence that He is God of my life? Then also, ask these questions about you, as a marriage. Do we seek God together? Together do we ask for help and guidance? Together do we seek and worship Him?

The other litmus test for a person or a marriage, as to whether God alone is God, is obedience. Do we do His will or our will? For me, this alone tells me if I have any other God than God. As a marriage if and when we know His will and we do it, we are confident we have no other Gods but God.

#2 *You shall not make for yourself an idol in the form of anything in heaven above or on the earth beneath or in the waters below. You shall not bow down to them or worship them; for I, the LORD your God, am a jealous God, punishing the children for the sin of the fathers to the third and fourth generation of those who hate me, but showing love to a thousand (generations) of those who love me and keep my commandments.*

Now I really don't expect many people reading this to have physical idol problems. I don't believe many westerners believe idols have powers, or that you would find many Christian couples bowing down or chanting to some object.

However, let me suggest an idol I have seen in western culture that often competes for worship, even among Christians. It's the idol of me, myself, and I. When someone worships this idol, so much gets measured by their perceived strengths or abilities. This person or marriage can become so self-reliant that it doesn't need God.

This couple can rely on their smartness, wealth, success or abilities to manipulate others. They have created systems in their life or beliefs that don't permit God to be God. This couple may be religious, but intimacy with God is absent. They talk about God, but rarely hear God talk to them. This self-sufficiency is the idol I see couples get into.

Interestingly in this command you see God describe

a relationship with Him. You as a person or a couple love him or hate him. This seems strong, but I think throughout the Bible you see this belief of not being able to serve two masters. You will love one and hate the other. In Revelation God says, " I wish you were cold or hot."

Hot pursuit of God is the only guaranteed solution of not having idols. Having idols can make you believe in your superiority in some way. This kind of self-worship can damage a marriage. I find couples with no self-worship are humble, teachable, and able to extend grace to themselves and their spouse as a lifestyle. The couple with no idols is a trinity with a sweet fragrance for sure.

#3 You shall not misuse the name of the LORD your God, for the LORD will not hold anyone guiltless who misuses His name.

The name of the Lord is to be held in high esteem. When God is the third person in your marriage you hold Him in a respectful place. This is totally a heart issue. When we value who He is, we value His name. I value Lisa and my children. If I hit a hammer on my hand I don't cry out Lisa, Lisa, Lisa in a derogatory or cursing manner as if she is to blame, or is to be a curse word to me. Actually no name we respect should be used as a curse word or in a derogatory manner.

Take this to marriage, not just with God's name but our spouse's as well, even our children. What if we valued them enough that even when we are mad at them we couldn't bring ourselves to curse them? That's the spirit God wants us to have towards Him and our spouse.

A spirit that says I give you reverence and honor above all in my life. That heart will find it difficult to curse God, even on a really bad day. The heart of reverence toward our spouse because they are God's child, bought by the sacrifice of Christ, can stop many inappropriate thoughts or words to our spouse. Again, I think questions help us probe ourselves or our marriage in regards to this commandment. Do we put our spouse down? Shame them? Treat them in word or deed like we are superior? Do we use foul language directly to them? Are they the brunt of our jokes? Is there a general attitude of resentment or disrespect?

A marriage honoring each other can easily be manifested by the tone of our love, as well as the glares or words we use. God is calling us in this trinity to believe our spouse is worthy of honor, and to speak and behave as if their worth is innate and unchangeable.

So far in these top three commandments there is

a theme. He is God, there is no other and respect Him. These commandments provide an atmosphere in a marriage. This is an atmosphere that loves God, knows that they both are dependent and in anticipation of God with a great respect for Him.

I travel to churches all the time preaching and doing various conferences. I have been to churches where the atmosphere is so charged with the worship, love and respect of God, you can feel God's presence and favor in that place. I think that the presence of God is what happens when a couple walks in this heart attitude toward God and each other. You can feel God in their trinity and that's a beautiful experience in a marriage.

#4 Remember the Sabbath day by keeping it holy. Six days you shall labor and do all your work, but the seventh day is a Sabbath to the LORD your God. On it you shall not do

any work, neither you, nor your son or daughter, nor your manservant or maidservant, nor your animals, nor the alien within your gates. For in six days the LORD made the heavens and the earth, the sea, and all that is in them, but he rested on the seventh day. Therefore the LORD blessed the Sabbath day and made it holy.

I have taught and researched this command quite a bit. I find that this is the only command that starts off with the word remember. This principle had existed before the law. This was a reminder to God's people to keep doing life this way.

They were to work hard and rest well. Doing nothing is challenging, especially for us Type A westerners. However, the person and marriage that does rest has created time for intentional relating. You can give time, attention, and affection to your spouse and family during this day.

This principle of rest is important so you both can recharge yourselves. You both are about doing so much in life, so stopping and breathing allows you to fortify yourself and each other as you do marriage, family, work, and life together. When you rest, you trust God. You can seek Him. A marriage that regularly obeys the command to rest will be less likely to burn out and behave poorly toward each other.

I am a strong believer in rest. I work hard but I rest well. I can feel if I start violating the Sabbath day. How do you and your marriage do with the Sabbath principle? How do you know if you're resting? How do you both recharge? What are the symptoms of each of you when you don't rest? If someone was watching your Sabbath would they be able to prove you were trying to rest?

Adding intentional, consistent rest to your marriage can sustain your marriage over the decades. Doing nothing regularly is a plan to stay more content and relaxed in life and in marriage.

#5 *Honor your father and your mother, so that you may live long in the land the LORD your God is giving you.*

Here is the commandment with a promise of a long life. I think generally most of us try to honor our parents. If you are fortunate to have had godly, loving, selfless parents, this commandment is easy. They have earned a place of honor and respect. In this situation it would be rational to respect them and allow their life and voice to have an influence in your life.

As a counselor I know that many people reading this page had parents that were not good parents, role models or in some cases, even respectable people. You may have been neglected, abused, abandoned, not heard or not encouraged. These parents are harder to honor, they may have offended your spouse, or even may have been a source of pain in your marriage.

Here you can do what you can to honor. As adults you are not required to obey your parents, but honor them. You and your spouse can negotiate the appropriate boundaries that can be managed and still attempt an atmosphere of honor. Two hearts committed to the principle of honor will bring more peace to your miracle of marriage.

#6 You shall not murder.

I doubt you struggle with direct threats of murdering your spouse. I'm not saying you never have had ill thoughts toward your spouse. I would, however, look at this commandment in the context of marriage in a couple of ways.

In the New Testament in First John he talked about if you hate your brother you are a murderer (3:15). Some of us are capable of not only feeling hate, but holding onto hatred. This holding of hatred toward anyone strangles or kills a relationship. The person with hatred becomes toxic and can only see the negative or the flaws of the other person. This kind of hatred is not acceptable in a marriage with God and your spouse.

The other way to apply this commandment to not murder is to evaluate our hearts toward our spouse's dream. Do we blow wind into our spouse to cheerlead them to fulfill their dreams, their destiny or callings? If you are guilty of empowering your spouse and sacrificing for their dreams, that is awesome.

The spouse, man or woman, who goes about blocking, sabotaging, or killing the dreams in their spouse's heart could be guilty of murdering a dream. In our marriage, our calling is to serve the other person and help them fulfill their dreams. I have a great example of my wife in this area. For most of our marriage, Lisa has worked in our office doing the labor of administrating, managing and improving my dreams. She has consistently allowed me to dream, even when the dream would show up on her desk as work. My dreams keep growing and my Lisa's support is still as strong as it was over twenty years ago.

I have seen men and women with opposite stories. Their spouse wouldn't let them dream, nor did they help them with their dream. They murdered the dream of their spouse. Murdering dreams can create pain, frustration, and resentment to grow in a marriage. So if this is a pattern, start writing a new chapter as a dream builder, so you're following the life commandment of giving life to your spouse and their dreams.

#7 You shall not commit adultery.

I wish I could just skip this verse completely because Christians just don't do this adultery behavior. Sadly, men and women who are Christians are cheating in record numbers. The Internet and social media like Facebook have lead people back to old relationships, as well as to new relationships, pornography and sexual services.

It's true, our culture now promotes sex outside of marriage. It's true, that many men are sex addicts in the church. It's true, both men and women who are Christians are watching porn or having inappropriate relationships via the Internet, cell phones, texting and every other way to connect two people.

Adultery is with us until the end of time; however, it doesn't have to be a part of your story or legacy. If it is already, God forgives; get professional help and heal your redemption story. Adultery is always a choice. I find many people who commit adultery never really decided not to commit adultery. They assumed they wouldn't, but never did they decide deep in their heart that it isn't an option. So the first stop to preventing adultery is before the Lord. Decide deeply that you are committed to fidelity and against ever committing adultery.

Once that decision is made, adding the boundaries around entertainment, pornography, the opposite sex, and the Internet are natural steps to take. Eliminate sexual entertainment, put porn blockers on your phone and computer, and have same sex accountability for your boundaries. Keep honest with your spouse about these boundaries and infractions regularly. These boundaries are agreed upon for both spouses.

If sex addiction is an issue, I recommend my books

The Final Freedom (Discovery Press, 2008), 101 Freedom Exercises (Discovery Press, 2009) and scheduling a free assessment to know what type of sex addict you are so you can be successful in recovery. If you're a wife of a sex addict, there are materials, phone support groups, and free assessments for you as well by calling Heart to Heart Counseling Center at 719-278-3708.

For more than twenty years I have had someone in my office almost weekly who has committed adultery and most of them are Christians. I have never heard them say it was worth it or they would do it again. They also believed they wouldn't get caught, but they all did. If this is an issue, get real help and heal.

Your miracle of marriage deserves both of you to value faithfulness. I know I value knowing Lisa would never cheat on me, and she knows I would not cheat on her and bring that pain into our family. This commandment to be faithful leaves a great legacy for your children. The fragrance of fidelity is awesome in this miracle of marriage.

#8 You shall not steal.

Again, I hope none of you have difficulty stealing things from others. Most of us grow out of this, if it's an issue earlier in life. I like to think of how stealing in a marriage is more like taking credit for things that, in all honesty, God and my spouse have made great contributions and responsibility toward.

Let me give you an example. I have two great children. Hadassah now seventeen went to state in debate and is a varsity cheerleader. Jubal is fifteen with two black belts and is a varsity football player. Both of my children have committed themselves to sexual purity.

Stealing would be if I took full credit for my children. There is no way I am totally responsible for all they are becoming. Firstly, God created them and speaks to them. My wife is a godly example and selflessly lives toward them. They have always gone to a good church and had excellent youth pastors, as well as attended a Christian school. This whole team of people gets credit for them becoming who they are. So often in marriage and life we want to take credit for what God does or what others have helped us to become or accomplish. I believe God and others get the praise for much of what has occurred in my life. My marriage is a team accomplishment: God, Lisa, myself, church, books, friends and family members as well.

Stealing in a marriage is when you believe or behave that you have more to do with the good in your life than is actually true. I think the life commandment here is to give praise and honor to your spouse regularly so they are acknowledged for the great contributions they are making in your life.

#9 You shall not give false testimony against your neighbor.

I love this commandment as well. It's like God is saying don't lie and don't tell stories about each other. It almost feels like a kindergarten teacher saying class, don't make things up about each other.

I realize this is talking maybe more in a legal sense of don't falsely accuse, falsify the facts in an accusation against anyone at anytime. However, in working with couples, I find that sometimes spouses have stories about each other that are not true.

I'll give you an example about when Lisa used to lose her keys. This was a frequent occurrence, and went on for a few years. We would look for the keys and eventually, I honestly refused to help look for the keys. Years when by and I was still talking about this, and Lisa appropriately challenged me to remember the last time she couldn't find her keys. I had to admit it had been years.

I still believed something that was no longer factually true. Lisa solved that issue years ago, but I was looking at a photograph as if it was permanent. Lisa is a continuous movie, not a photograph. She continues to grow and amaze me.

If I, however, keep a photograph of a fault and believe it to be true, I will be falsely accusing her in my mind. I will keep a judgment that is not only unfair, it is simply not true anymore.

I have seen so many couples hold a past photograph for years, bearing false witness toward their spouse when actually it's been five, ten, sometimes decades since that fact has reoccurred. What happens to this spouse with the photograph is that their false judgment of their spouse keeps them stuck in their relationship.

An example of this would be relating to your thirty year old child based on something they did as a teenager. That sounds crazy, but if we hold on to past judgments of our spouse, we are doing this crazy behavior which makes for some interesting conversations.

If you struggle with false accusations of your spouse, make a list of them. Then take the list and factually put them in time. If it has been a while, then ask them to forgive you of these false accusations that you have in your heart and mind, and pray together to have these removed from your marriage.

I also recommend that you regularly praise your spouse about overcoming in this area to reinforce the current reality of your spouse. You'll be amazed at how much more positively you can see your spouse.

#10 *You shall not covet your neighbor's house. You shall not covet your neighbor's wife, or his manservant or maidservant, his ox or donkey or anything that belongs to your neighbor.*

This final commandment about being content is really funny to me. God asks us not to lust after or desire other people's relationships, successes or stuff. I am really glad he added the phrase "or anything that belongs to your neighbor." He knew there would be an evolution of gadgets that could tempt us to envy our neighbor in the future.

Here is how I have settled this issue. I believe God has an inheritance for each of us. I believe my inheritance is mine and yours is yours. My house is perfect for me and yours is perfect for you. Your spouse is a perfect mate for you, as Lisa is for me. My business and ministry is my inheritance, as yours is for you. Your toys are your toys, and my toys are my toys from God. As long as I don't worship the toys, I can have what God allows and the same goes for everyone.

Lust and envy of the Joneses is insidious and says to God that my inheritance isn't good enough. The factors of preparation, responsibility, saving, investing, and obedience can all be factors as to where we currently are. However, God is the giver of inheritances and He decides to expand our inheritance throughout our lives.

I am content. Contentment dissolves issues of envy or lusting after other people or things. Contentment gives you the positives of what and who is in your life. Discontentment makes you focus on what you don't believe you have and makes you less grateful, regardless of your level of prosperity.

In a marriage, contentment provides a great environment. Contentment brings gratefulness and praise to the party of your life. Honestly, most of us are not worthy of the blessings we have. I know where God has brought me from, so I am so grateful for the blessings in my life today.

I find content people are aware of how blessed their life is by God. Those who covet feel and act as if God has cursed them because they don't have someone or something different. I would encourage you as a couple, that if ungratefulness has crept into the marriage, ask God and your spouse for forgiveness and then practice intentional gratefulness.

I often thank God for where I live, for my spouse, kids, even my dog, vehicles, my business, and my co-workers who make so much happen in our business.

Gratefulness is a key sign that you and your marriage are keeping this last commandment.

I hope you enjoyed this jaunt through the Ten Commandments for marriage. I find it helpful to apply these heartbeats of our Father to His final creation called marriage.

Appendix

Feelings Exercise

1. I feel (put feeling word here) when (put a present situation).
2. I first remember feeling (put the same feeling word here) when (explain earliest occurrence of this feeling).

Abandoned	Argumentative	Burned	Crabby	Disenchanted
Abused	Aroused	Callous	Cranky	Disgusted
Aching	Astonished	Calm	Crazy	Disinterested
Accepted	Assertive	Capable	Creative	Dispirited
Accused	Attached	Captivated	Critical	Distressed
Accepting	Attacked	Carefree	Criticized	Distrustful
Admired	Attentive	Careful	Cross	Distrusted
Adored	Attractive	Careless	Crushed	Disturbed
Adventurous	Aware	Caring	Cuddly	Dominated
Affectionate	Awestruck	Cautious	Curious	Domineering
Agony	Badgered	Certain	Cut	Doomed
Alienated	Baited	Chased	Damned	Doubtful
Aloof	Bashful	Cheated	Dangerous	Dreadful
Aggravated	Battered	Cheerful	Daring	Eager
Agreeable	Beaten	Childlike	Dead	Ecstatic
Aggressive	Beautiful	Choked Up	Deceived	Edgy
Alive	Belligerent	Close	Deceptive	Edified
Alone	Belittled	Cold	Defensive	Elated
Alluring	Bereaved	Comfortable	Delicate	Embarrassed
Amazed	Betrayed	Comforted	Delighted	Empowered
Amused	Bewildered	Competent	Demeaned	Empty
Angry	Blamed	Competitive	Demoralized	Enraged
Anguished	Blaming	Complacent	Dependent	Enraptured
Annoyed	Bonded	Complete	Depressed	Enthusiastic
Anxious	Bored	Confident	Deprived	Enticed
Apart	Bothered	Confused	Deserted	Esteemed
Apathetic	Brave	Considerate	Desirable	Exasperated
Apologetic	Breathless	Consumed	Desired	Excited
Appreciated	Bristling	Content	Despair	Exhilarated
Appreciative	Broken-up	Cool	Despondent	Exposed
Apprehensive	Bruised	Courageous	Destroyed	Fake
Appropriate	Bubbly	Courteous	Different	Fascinated
Approved	Burdened	Coy	Dirty	Feisty

Ferocious, Foolish, Forced, Forceful, Forgiven, Forgotten, Free, Friendly, Frightened, Frustrated, Full, Funny, Furious, Gay, Generous, Grouchy, Grumpy, Hard, Harried, Hassled, Healthy, Helpful, Helpless, Hesitant, High, Hollow, Honest, Hopeful, Hopeless, Horrified, Hostile, Humiliated, Hurried, Hurt, Hyper, Ignorant, Joyous, Lively,

Lonely, Loose, Lost, Loving, Low, Lucky, Lustful, Mad, Maudlin, Malicious, Mean, Miserable, Misunderstood, Moody, Morose, Mournful, Mystified, Nasty, Nervous, Nice, Numb, Nurtured, Nuts, Obsessed, Offended, Open, Ornery, Out of control, Overcome, Overjoyed, Overpowered, Overwhelmed, Pampered, Panicked, Paralyzed, Paranoid,

Patient, Peaceful, Pensive, Perceptive, Perturbed, Phony, Pleasant, Pleased, Positive, Powerless, Present, Precious, Pressured, Pretty, Proud, Pulled apart, Put down, Puzzled, Quarrelsome, Queer, Quiet, Raped, Ravished, Ravishing, Real, Refreshed, Regretful, Rejected, Rejuvenated, Rejecting, Relaxed, Relieved, Remarkable, Remembered, Removed, Repulsed, Repulsive, Resentful,

Resistant, Responsible, Responsive, Repressed, Respected, Restless, Revolved, Riled, Rotten, Ruined, Sad, Safe, Satiated, Satisfied, Scared, Scolded, Scorned, Scrutinized, Secure, Seduced, Seductive, Self-centered, Self-conscious, Selfish, Separated, Sensuous, Sexy, Shattered, Shocked, Shot down, Shy, Sickened, Silly, Sincere, Sinking, Smart, Smothered,

Smug, Sneaky, Snowed, Soft, Solid, Solitary, Sorry, Spacey, Special, Spiteful, Spontaneous, Squelched, Starved, Stiff, Stimulated, Stifled, Strangled, Strong, Stubborn, Stuck, Stunned, Stupid, Subdued, Submissive, Successful, Suffocated, Sure, Sweet, Sympathy, Tainted, Tearful, Tender, Tense, Terrific, Terrified, Thrilled, Ticked, Tickled

Tight
Timid
Tired
Tolerant
Tormented
Torn
Tortured
Touched
Trapped
Tremendous
Tricked
Trusted
Trustful
Trusting
Ugly
Unacceptable
Unapproachable
Unaware
Uncertain
Uncomfortable
Under control
Understanding
Understood
Undesirable
Unfriendly
Ungrateful
Unified
Unhappy
Unimpressed
Unsafe
Unstable
Upset
Uptight
Used
Useful

Useless
Unworthy
Validated
Valuable
Valued
Victorious
Violated
Violent
Voluptuous
Vulnerable
Warm
Wary
Weak
Whipped
Whole
Wicked
Wild
Willing
Wiped out
Wishful
Withdrawn
Wonderful
Worried
Worthy

Guideline 1:
No Examples about Each Other

Guideline 2:
Maintain Eye Contact

Guideline 3:
No Feedback

Resources by Dr. Doug Weiss

Marriage

Miracle of Marriage Vol. 1 (DVD—$29.95)
The Miracle of Marriage is an amazing journey for couples of small groups. In Volume One, Dr. Weiss introduces couples to the foundational revelation of marriage.

The Ten-Minute Marriage Principle (Book—$14.99)
By taking just ten minutes a day to focus on each other, you can enhance your marriage in ways you'll appreciate for a lifetime. As you and your spouse learn to talk and understand each other more fully, you'll ignite true, lasting intimacy.

Intimacy: A 100 Day Guide to Lasting Relationships (Book—$11.99)
Dr. Weiss walks couples through the skills necessary for lifelong intimate relationships. This guide can transform couples to deeper levels of intimacy.

The 7 Love Agreements (Book—$13.99, DVD $12.95)
These seven agreements are so powerful only one person needs to apply them to see a marriage make progress. Weiss explains the power of agreement in the areas of faithfulness, patience, forgiveness, service, respect, kindness and celebration.

Winning @ Marriage (DVD—$69.00)
This three-DVD, 4 1/2 hour marriage conference is for everybody. You will gain insight, laugh and most importantly walk through the practical tools to make your marriage a winning marriage.

The Best Sex of Your Life, For Men or Women (DVD—$29.95 Each)
This video is a must for every Christian man or woman. You are practically and passionately walked through Christian sexuality that really works. For over a decade, couples have been using these principles and techniques to radically improve their love life.

How to Really Love a Woman (DVD—$69.00)
In this 12 part DVD series, you will be exposed to tried and true principles to help you learn how to really love a woman. These 30 minute sessions are easily and immediately applicable. Begin to love your spouse the way you wished you could. Dr. Weiss' practical tools will make you more successful at loving your spouse.

Men's Recovery

The Final Freedom (Book—$22.95, CD—$35.00)
Plentiful, current information on sexual addiction and recovery that goes beyond what many counselors can offer. Many attest to successful recovery from this product alone.

101 Freedom Exercises for Sexual Addiction Recovery (Workbook—$39.95)
Proven techniques Dr. Weiss has recommended through the years to successfully help thousands gain and maintain recovery from sexual addiction. A Christian Edition of 101 Practical Exercises

Steps to Freedom: A Christian 12-Step Guide (Workbook—$14.95)
This is a thorough interaction with the Twelve Steps of recovery from a Christian perspective. This workbook can be used in Twelve-Step study groups or for individual use.

Sex, Men and God (Book—$13.99, CD—$29.95)
Finally, an encouraging message for men who want to be sexually successful! God is not against sexual pleasure in your marriage! In fact, He created it! So what is keeping you from experiencing the best of His creation? This book has clearly and creatively outlined practical, doable suggestions and principles that will help you enjoy your sexuality as God intended.

Helping Her Heal (DVD—$69.00)
This two hour DVD is essential for the addict who has exposed his wife to his sexual addiction. Dr. Weiss clearly shares teh effects on an addict's wife and her world when sex addiction is identified.

Why Men Lie (DVD—$44.95)
In this DVD set Dr. Weiss will expose the viewer to specific reasons

as to why men lie and the helpful strategies to end the lying. This set shines light into the mind and heart of men that lie.

6 Types of Sex Addicts (CD—$29.95)
This CD will give you more information than most therapists have on sexual addiction. You will be able to finally know how you became a sex addict and identify why you might still be relapsing. A must for every sex addict in recovery!

Treatment for the 6 Types of Sex Addicts (CD—$29.95)
This CD will take you to the next level in your recovery. Once you know the type of sex addict you are, Dr. Doug outlines the same treatment plan you would receive in an individual session.

Addict to Addict (DVD—$29.95)
This amazing DVD has 8 addicts telling their stories through directed questions. These individuals address key issues along with their journey through recovery. A must DVD for every sex addict.

Women's Recovery

Partners: Healing from his Addiction (Book—$14.95)
This book has the latest research on the effects to partners of sex addicts. Riveting statistics are combined with personal stories of partners in recovery.

Partner's Recovery Guide: 100 Empowering Exercises (Workbook—$39.95)
This is the most practical workbook for partners and was conceived from many years of successful treatment for partners of sex addicts. It includes 100 proven techniques used in counseling sessions to help partners.

Beyond Love: 12-Step Recovery Guide for Partners (Workbook—$14.95)
This is an interactive workbook that allows the partner to gain insight and strength through working the Twelve Steps. This book can be used individually or as a group step-study workbook.

Calming the Storm of Anger (DVD—$29.95)
This DVD is applicable for women who have just experienced disclosure or if disclosure was years ago. If anger is an issue for you, be sure to address this so you can heal.

Now That I Know, What Should I Do? (DVD—$69.00)
This DVD answers the ten most frequently asked questions by partners who have just found out about their spouse's sexual addiction.

Partner to Partner (DVD—$19.95)
This DVD is a dialogue of several partners of sex addicts sharing their hope and experience. These women address key issues facing a partner of a sex addict and their journey through recovery.

Intimacy Anorexia Recovery

Intimacy Anorexia (DVD—$69.95)
This DVD explains the age old question, "Why doesn't my partner want to be intimacy with me?" It includes 90 minutes of up-to-date information on sexual, emotional and spiritual anorexia and can open new insights for individuals or couples to begin a life of intimacy. This DVD will give you the characteristics, causes and strategies of intimacy anorexia. This DVD also provides solutions for the intimacy anorexic to start their road to recovery.

Married and Alone (DVD—$49.95)
This DVD is for the spouse of an intimacy/sexual anorexic. You feel disconnected, untouched and often unloved. You are not crazy and Dr. Weiss will help you to start a journey of recovery from living with a spouse with intimacy/sexual anorexia.

Intimacy Anorexia-The Book (Book—$22.95)
This is the first book to address intimacy anorexia. Regardless if you are the anorexic or the spouse you will learn the characteristics, strategies and patterns of intimacy anorexia. You will also be introduced to why intimacy anorexia is an addiction as well as the beginning steps to recovery for the intimacy anorexic

Intimacy Anorexia-The Workbook (Workbook—$39.95)
This is like therapy in a box. You will be exposed to over 100 exercises that have already been proven helpful in Dr. Weiss' practice of treating intimacy anorexia step by step the anorexia is taken from withholding intimacy to be able to give intimacy if they do these crucial exercises

Intimacy Anorexia-The Steps (Workbook—$14.95)
The twelve steps have helped millions heal from many types of addiction. This is the only twelve step workbook just for intimacy anorexia. Each step give you progress in you healing from intimacy anorexia.

Married and Alone-Healing Exercises for Spouses (Workbook—$39.95)
This guide will help bring about healing for those impacted by their spouse's intimacy anorexic behavior. This si teh first workbook to offer practical suggestions and techniques to better navigate through this recovery

Married and Alone-The Twelve Step Guide (Workbook—$14.95)
This book follows in the tradition of the Twelve-Steps by breaking down the various principles for each reader so that they can experience teh discovery of the Twelve-Step promises

Other Resources

Beyond the Bedroom (Book—$14.95)
This is the first book to discuss the issues of adult children of sex addicts, as well as provides a road map to recovery. You will also be exposed to research findings on the impact of being a child of a sexual addict.

Get a Grip: How to Turn Your Worst Behaviors into Strengths (Book—$19.99)
This book will take you from having behaviors control you into learning how to control your behaviors. This book is packed with helpful information for anyone struggling with a behavior that seems to be controlling them. This step-by-step process can help you go from repeat failure to success.

The Power of Pleasure (Book—$14.95, CD—$14.95)
Knowing how you are created for pleasure is pivotal in having happiness. Your pleasure zones and hierarchy are as unique as you are. This book unlocks your ability to have a life full of your pleasures.

ITEM	QUAN	PRICE	TOTAL
Miracle of Marriage Vol. 1	_____	29.95	_____
The Ten-Minute Marriage Principle	_____	14.99	_____
Intimacy: A 100 Day Guide to Lasting Relationships	_____	11.99	_____
The 7 Love Agreements Book	_____	13.99	_____
The 7 Love Agreements DVD	_____	12.95	_____
Winning @ Marriage	_____	69.00	_____
The Best Sex of Your Life for Men Only	_____	29.95	_____
The Best Sex of Your Life for Women Only	_____	29.95	_____
How to Really Love a Woman	_____	69.00	_____
The Final Freedom Book	_____	22.95	_____
The Final Freedom CD	_____	35.00	_____
101 Freedom Exercises for Sex Addiction Recovery	_____	39.95	_____
Steps to Freedom	_____	14.95	_____
Sex, Men and God Book	_____	13.99	_____
Sex, Men and God CD	_____	29.95	_____
Helping Her Heal	_____	69.00	_____
Why Men Lie	_____	44.95	_____
6 Types of Sex Addicts	_____	29.95	_____
Treatment for the 6 Types of Sex Addicts	_____	29.95	_____
Addict to Addict	_____	19.95	_____
Partners: Healing from His Addiction	_____	14.95	_____
Partner's Recovery Guide: 100 Empowering Exercises	_____	39.95	_____
Beyond Love	_____	14.95	_____
Calming the Storm of Anger	_____	29.95	_____
Now That I Know, What Should I Do?	_____	69.95	_____
Partner to Partner	_____	19.95	_____
Intimacy Anorexia DVD	_____	69.95	_____
Married and Alone DVD	_____	49.95	_____
Intimacy Anorexia-The Book	_____	22.95	_____
Intimacy Anorexia-The Workbook	_____	39.95	_____
Intimacy Anorexia-The Steps	_____	14.95	_____
Married and Alone: Healing Exercises for Spouses	_____	39.95	_____
Married and Alone: The Twelve Step Guide	_____	14.95	_____

Beyond the Bedroom	_____	14.95 ____
Get a Grip	_____	19.99 ____
The Power of Pleasure Book	_____	14.95 ____
The Power of Pleasure CD	_____	29.95 ____

Sub Total
7.4% Sales Tax (inColorado only)
Shipping/Handling-add $8 + 1 for each additional item (in USA)
Shipping/Handling-add $30 + $1 for each additional item (outside USA)

Total _____

VISA/MC/DISCOVER # _____ EXP DATE _____

NAME _____ SIGNATURE _____

ADDRESS _____ CITY ____ _____

STATE _____ ZIP CODE _____ PHONE (_____)_____

MAIL: Heart to Heart Counseling Centers, P.O. Box 51055,
Colorado Springs, CO 80949
E-MAIL: heart2heart@xc.org Website: www.drdougweiss.com

719.278.3708

(Make Checks payable to Heart to Heart Counseling Center)

318 Miracle of Marriage

Telephone Counseling

Telephone counseling is convenient and effective.

Individual Telephone Counseling - Individual counseling offers a personal treatment plan for successful healing in your life by telephone. A counselor can help you understand how you became stuck and gvie strategies for you to begin your road to recovery.

Couple Telephone Counseling - Couples are helped through critical issues in thier marrige due to the intimacy anorexia of one or both people in the marriage. We have helped many couples rebuild their relationship, as they begin to understand and implement the necessary skills for an intimate relationship.

Partner Telephone Counseling - Partners of intimacy anorexics need an advocate to call upon. Feelings of fear, hurt, anger, betrayal, and grief require a compassionate, effective response. We provide that expert guidance and direction. We have helped many partners heal from the side effects of living with an intimacy anorexic. A phone appointment today can begin your personal journey toward healing.

Call Heart to Heart Counseling Center at (719) 278-3708 to schedule your telephone appointment today.

3-Day Intensive

Sexual Addiction Couple Intensive

This intensive serves the needs of couples who are trapped within the disease of sex addiction. A master's level counselor will address the structural damage, which takes place in most systems within sexually addictive relationships. The couple will attain skills and goals in order to count themselves among the many clients who have successfully remained in committed relationships after the awareness of sexual addiction. A new beginning is possible with the tools attained from this intensive. This intensive includes
one counseling session for the addict, one session for the partner and one session for the couple with a licensed counselor each day, Structured assignments are given to work on during your own time. Attendance is encouraged in our office Freedom Groups and Partner's support groups in the evening. The Sexual

Addiction Couple's 3-Day Intensives held at Heart to Heart Counseling Center in Colorado Springs, Colorado is available most Mondays through Wednesdays. Call to schedule your intensive at (719) 278-3708.

Sexual Addiction Individual Intensive

Those struggling with sex addiction want solutions. This 3-day intensive focuses on solutions. Some highlights of this intensive will be:

- Discovering the origination of your sexual addiction
- Outlining a definitive plan for your recovery
- Identifying a working plan for deprivation
- Addressing core issues of sexual addiction

This solution-driven intensive can help make recovery smoother and much more attainable. This intensive would include one and a half sessions of individual counseling in the morning and one session of individual counseling in the afternoon. Structured assignments are given to work on during your own time. Attendance is encouraged in our office support groups in the evening. Sexual Addiction 3-Day Intensives held at Heart to Heart Counseling Center in Colorado Springs, Colorado are available most Mondays through Wednesdays.

Partner Intensive

If you are married or living with an intimacy anorexic or sexual addict, there are often residuals to this. The addict's addiction may have left you feeling hurt, betrayed, angry, confused or even hopeless. This 3-day intensive allows you to look at yourself, as well as the consequences of living with an intimacy anorexic or sexual addict. The skills you will learn can expedite your healing from the consequences of their addiction. You deserve to be all you can for the people in your life. This intensive can help you be your best again.

This solution-driven intensive can help make recovery smoother and much more attainable. This intensive would include one and a half sessions of individual counseling in the morning and one session of individual counseling in the afternoon. Structured assignments are given to work on during your own time. Attendance is encouraged in our office support groups in the evening. Partner 3-Day Intensives held at Heart to Heart Counseling Center in Colorado Springs, Colorado are available most Mondays through Wednesdays.

Intimacy Anorexia Couple Intensive

This intensive serves the needs of couples who are strugging with one or both having intimcy anorexia issues. A master's level counselor will address the structural damage, which takes place in most systems. The couple will attain skills and goals in order to count themselves among the many clients who have successfully remained in committed relationships after the awareness of intimacy anorexia. A new beginning is possible with the tools attained from this intensive. This intensive includes one counseling session for him, one session for her and one session for the couple with a licensed counselor each day. Structured assignments are given to work on during your own time. Attendance is encouraged in our office Intimacy Anorexia Groups and Partner's support groups in the evening. The Intimacy Anorexia Couple's 3-Day Intensives held at Heart to Heart Counseling Center in Colorado Springs, Colorado is available most Mondays through Wednesdays. Call to schedule your intensive at (719) 278-3708.

NOTE: If you need to schedule an intensive with Dr. Weiss immediately and cannot wait until the next scheduled appointment, you may be able to schedule an Emergency Intensive. Call to request an Emergency Intensive, which is priced at a higher rate than the others.

Adult Child of Sexual Addict Intensive

This 3-day intensive will help anyone who grew up in a home that was tainted by the colors of a sexual addict. Whether it was your mom or dad, you will be able to practically deal with your anger, hurt, betrayal and other issues involved from living with a sexually addicted parent.

Teenaged Child of a Sexual Addict Intensive

Most of us are aware teens are affected by a parent's sexual addiction. If your adolescent is experiencing symptoms from living with a sexually addicted parent in the past or present there is help. This 3-day intensive can help teens with emotions, pain, anger and the hurt related to the confusion of living with a sexually addicted parent. Teenaged Child of a Sexual Addict 3-Day Intensives held at Heart to Heart Counseling Center in Colorado Springs, Colorado are available most Mondays through Wednesdays.

Sex Abuse Intensive

This 3-day intensive addresses the residual affects of sexual abuse, which many sex addicts and partners experienced. This intensive focuses on giving relief of the symptoms due to the sexual abuse. Sex Abuse 3-Day Intensives held at Heart to Heart Counseling Center in Colorado Springs, Colorado are available most Mondays through Wednesdays. Schedule your Intensive Today by calling (719) 278-3708.

American Association for Sex Addiction Therapy

Dr. Weiss has created a 45-hour program to train counselors how to work with sexual addicts and partners of sexual addicts. This DVD/Workbook training set is available for anyone who would like to have more information on treating sexual addiction. Everyone who completes this 45-hour course will receive a certificate of completion. This course is for anyone who has a significant interest in the field of sexual addiction. This course can be taken by anyone who wants to increase their knowledge of sex addiction and partner's recovery.

This course is also part of certifying licensed counselors to become certified as a Sexual Recovery Therapist (SRT). If you or a counselor you know has an interest in treating sexual addicts or their spouses call the phone number below.

For more information or to place an order, please call

(719) 330-2425

or visit www.aasat.org